The Playbook

6 Strategies to Finish Strong for Christ

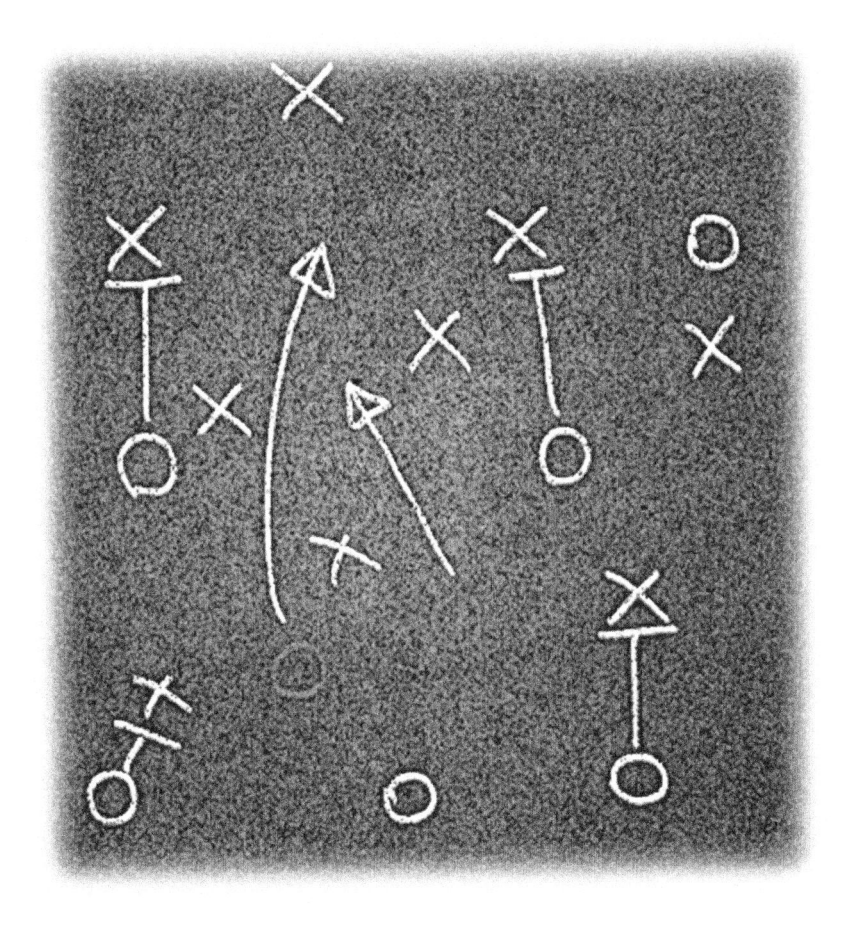

James Dickey

Copyright © 2019 by James Dickey
All rights reserved.
Printed in the United States of America

Any use of content without the written permission of the author is prohibited.

Unless otherwise indicated, all Scripture quotations are taken from the Holy Bible, New Living Translation, copyright © 1996, 2004, 2015 by Tyndale House Foundation. Used by permission of Tyndale House Publishers, Inc., Carol Stream, Illinois 60188. All rights reserved.

Scripture taken from the New King James Version®. Copyright © 1982 by Thomas Nelson. Used by permission. All rights reserved.

GOD'S WORD is a copyrighted work of God's Word to the Nations. Quotations are used by permission. Copyright 1995 by God's Word to the Nations. All rights reserved.

Table Of Contents

	Page
Introduction	*4*
Strategy #1	*11*
Strategy #2	*32*
Strategy #3	*46*
Strategy #4	*70*
Strategy #5	*87*
Strategy #6	*116*
Final Thoughts	*135*
Questions	*137*
Helpful Links	*142*

Introduction

I must admit, I am a football fan. College football in particular. If you've watched much football, you've probably noticed it. At the end of the 3rd Quarter, the players on both teams will often stretch a hand skyward with four fingers extended. Why do they do that? To remind one another that it's just the 4th Quarter! The game isn't over yet, so they can't take a break to rest or heal. Not yet. This is the time for them to recommit themselves to the task at hand. Winning a football game.

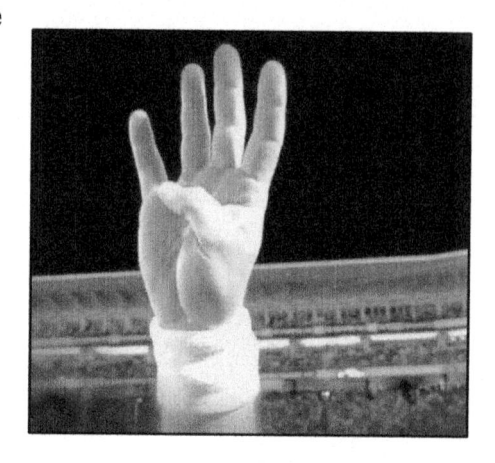

No football game is won or lost after just three quarters, nor should we imagine that life as a follower of Jesus Christ is any different. Maybe you've never been in a locker room or on a football field, but as faithful Christians we are in a contest – a battle for the souls of mankind. Our goal as the Church is to take the love and Gospel of Jesus Christ to a world that badly needs it. No matter who you are or how many days are behind you in your service for Christ, if your heart is still beating, the clock hasn't reached 0.00 yet.

Perhaps you're like me – when I look in the mirror, I can tell that more of my days to do ministry are behind me than in front of me. I've entered that period of life that could be termed MY "4th Quarter". Whether you're right there with me or you're not quite as old as I am, this may be the perfect time to develop your strategy for leaving an eternal legacy for the Kingdom of God.

> **You may be in your 20s or your 70s, but each of us is called by Christ to actively plan for this game we call "life".**

Our Playbook must contain strategies that are Biblical to be certain they will be successful. They must be practical, or we will fail to implement them. **The 4th Quarter Playbook** seeks to help you develop both.

For many adults that reach their 4th Quarter of life, their goal is to just sit down and take it easy, wanting only to do whatever they feel like doing whenever they feel like doing it. I get it. Years of working; bodies that don't feel as vibrant as they once did; dreams that have been postponed to raise families and meet responsibilities. Whether they say it out loud or not, 4th Quarter adults think, "This is MY time now!"

Unfortunately, lots of 4th Quarter adults feel the same about their efforts for the Kingdom of God. They spent years working in the nursery at church when their kids were young. They were the ones investing in youth programs, staffing VBS, and teaching Sunday School in churches all across our country. With many years of ministry behind them, they say to the church, and in a sense, to God Himself, "This is MY time now! Let some of the "younger ones" take care of that. I served my time."

Once again, I understand what you're feeling, but please take the next words you read to heart:

NOW is the BEST time to make the BIGGEST difference for the Kingdom of God.

This is that time in life when all the expectations of work and many of the hurdles involved in raising a family are beginning to ebb. This is when you get to write your own playbook for the future. Perhaps these **6 Strategies** can help you as you plan your direction for the years that lie ahead.

I've thought about what it means to be a 4th Quarter adult, and this is what I've discovered for me that I believe applies to you, as well.

- **I'm still important to the Kingdom of God.**
  My adoption into the family of God through Christ, and the Holy Spirit's empowering of me

for ministry do not come with an expiration date! I signed on for eternity, so I still matter to God and should have a part in building His kingdom.

- **God has spent a lifetime building His truth and values into my life.** What I know about life, the Bible, ministry, love, and forgiveness has been accumulated wisdom and knowledge over many decades. God didn't go to all that trouble equipping me for ministry to have me drop out once I reach a certain age. I'm more useful and valuable as a servant of the Most-High God than I've ever been!

- **This isn't the time for me to quit or sit.** I know that's what I feel like some days, but then I remember, it's just the 4th Quarter! There is much work to do. Jesus told His disciples that the *"fields are ripe and ready to harvest"* (*John 4:35*). He just needs workers to labor in the fields to reap what He has prepared. With work still to be completed, why would I expect to be excused from the labor for which I've been called and prepared?

- **This is when I need to be cementing the Legacy of Faith I'll be leaving behind.** Who have I impacted for Christ? Where have I invested the material wealth provided by God? The legacy of our lives is determined more by how we finish than by how we began. Ask yourself, **"What will be the last great work of**

your life before God calls you home?" Your answer will determine your Legacy of Faith.

In the Bible, James writes this:
How do you know what your life will be like tomorrow? Your life is like the morning fog – it's here a little while, then it's gone. James 4:14 NLT

Don't you agree? Life moves along pretty quickly. We find ourselves looking back at what we think were our most productive years, but it needn't be so! The Spirit didn't intend James' words to discourage us, but to MOTIVATE us. None of us knows what tomorrow will bring. That's why it's imperative that we make the most of each day we have.

Feeling selfish about your time as you sense your days going by too quickly and whatever dreams you had are dissipating as well? Jesus has a word for each of us:

If you try to hang on to your life, you will lose it. But if you give up your life for my sake and for the sake of the Good News, you will save it. Mark 8:35. NLT

Do you have any doubt that Jesus understood how precious life is? Every sunrise makes a difference, or at least it should. But the promise of the Messiah is that when we spend our lives on behalf of the

Kingdom and the Gospel, those days aren't gone, but rewarded by Him in heaven. Not a bad trade, right?

Jesus' admonition to us sure sounds like it was never His intention that we put our feet up on the couch or lean back in the recliner. Don't get me wrong – there's nothing sinful about wanting to have a little "me time" in the here-and-now. Spend a week beachcombing, go hiking in the Rockies and breathe the pine-scented air, or see if you can sink that 20-foot putt. We all need a break sometimes. But we were redeemed to be servants of the Lord Jesus Christ until He decides it's time for us to stop. If there's still time on the clock, the game isn't over.

4th Quarter adults are generally confronting the same issues. Will we have enough money in retirement; how do we deal with aging parents or kids that won't grow up; is anyone really going to care about us next month or next year? As **4th Quarter Teams** meet around the country in churches that have adopted our strategies, it's my hope you'll be a part. With the help of others, perhaps you can figure out how to fit in to what God is doing all around you. But more importantly, together we can help you understand better how to leave the spiritual Legacy you desire. And since you're reading this, YOU may be the person in your church that rallies others to Finish Strong for Christ after they assumed they were ready to ease off into the sunset.

Stay in the game! Don't quit now, it's just the 4th Quarter! Look over these 6 Strategies and use them to create your own 4th Quarter Playbook so YOU can Finish Strong.

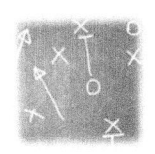

Strategy #1 – Never stop learning about, and growing in, your FAITH.

Why is this first strategy so important as you develop your 4th Quarter Playbook? Because no matter who you are and no matter how much you think you know about God, His love FOR you and His power at work IN you are limitless.

> Now all glory to God, who is able, through his mighty power at work **within us**, to accomplish **infinitely more** than we might ask or think. Ephesians 3:20 NLT

It's hard to imagine that a Holy God would look at sinful, feeble humanity and say, "I love you and I want you to be mine for eternity!" But that's exactly the reason He made us and then paid the ultimate price through His Son to redeem us from the penalty of our own sin, then gave us His Holy Spirit to empower us:

> Even **before He made the world, God loved us and chose us in Christ** to be holy and without fault in his eyes. God decided in advance **to adopt us into His own family by bringing us to Himself through Jesus Christ.** This is what He wanted to do, and **it gave Him great pleasure.**

*And **when you believed in Christ, He identified you as His own by giving you the Holy Spirit**, whom He promised long ago. The Spirit is **God's guarantee** that He will give us the inheritance He promised and that He has purchased us to be His own people. He did this so we would praise and glorify Him.*
Ephesians 1:4-5; 13-14. NLT

**God had a plan
and He executed it to perfection.**

How do we appropriate the gift of salvation through Christ and receive the promises of God?

The Beginning of Faith

At the very heart of our efforts for Jesus is our faith. Faith is what empowers us, encourages us, and motivates us. Faith is what allows us to see what we couldn't otherwise, to trust when it seems like there is no hope, and to believe God for what seems impossible. Without faith, we have nothing.

Jesus told Nicodemus in *John 3* that we must each be **"born again"**. We understand physical birth and so did Nicodemus. But Nicodemus was puzzled over exactly what Jesus meant by the term, "born again":

> *"What do you mean?" exclaimed Nicodemus. "How can an old man go back into his mother's womb and be born again?"*   John 3:4 NLT

Let me lay some foundation before I try to answer Nicodemus' question. We humans are **triune** in nature, made in the image of God. We're composed of a physical **body**; a **soul** that includes our mind, our will, and our emotions; and a **spirit** that, since Adam's sin, is dead to the things of God. This dead spirit is the price we pay for "Original Sin". No one since Adam and Eve has been born with a living spirit connected to God except for Jesus – one of the reasons He was virgin-born so He could escape the curse of Original Sin.

The spirit in all human beings is intended to commune with the Spirit of God in an intimate way.

> **The spirit in us is our means to connect with the Spirit in Him.**

Jesus enjoyed a perfect connection with the Father through the Spirit. That kind of intimacy with God is what we are offered through salvation.

That's exactly what Jesus was trying to make clear to Nicodemus:

> *Jesus replied, "I assure you, no one can enter the Kingdom of God without being born of*

water (this refers to human birth) *and the* **Spirit.** *John 3:5 NLT*

There is a moment when our spirits are brought back to life, allowing us to commune with the God of the universe Who made us. That event occurs at the **moment of salvation**, when individuals acknowledge their sin and seek forgiveness through the only One who can offer it. It's the moment evangelical Christians refer to as being "born again". At that moment, our spirits are brought back to life and become capable of relating directly to the Spirit of God. We are, at that very moment, adopted into God's own family to be His own people, as Paul described the event in the passage from *Ephesians 1* presented earlier.

Jesus explained our entry into eternal life this way:

> *"I tell you the truth, those who listen to my message and believe in God who sent me* **have eternal life.** *They will never be condemned for their sins, but they have* **already passed from death into life."**
> *John 5:24*

The following illustration shows that transition. All of us **begin life below the line.** Jesus invites us to live life **ABOVE the line.**

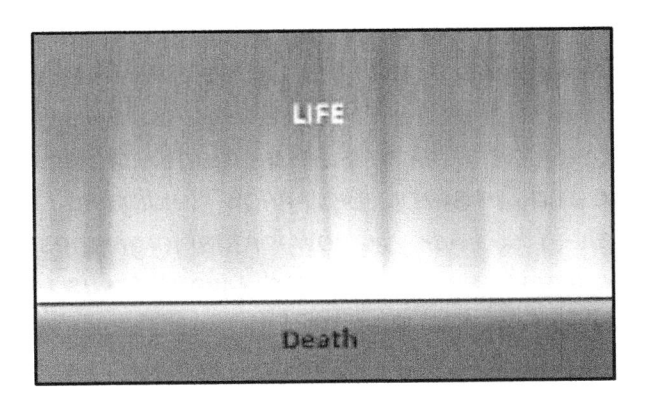

That's what the Good News is all about. When we accept the invitation that Jesus extends, we step from life that is the "best we can do" into an existence that will last for eternity. Kingdom life is what Jesus offers all of us. Life above the line – life lived to the fullest extent (*John 10:10*) – life that doesn't have to wait for "someday" to experience the joys of the Kingdom of God.

Who gets to pass from death to life across the bridge that Jesus built? Anyone may.

Only those with a heart to know God can. If you've never had that "moment" when you passed from death to life – that experience of being "born again" – God has been waiting for you to respond to Him. And while there are no magic words that will move you from below the line to the abundant life above it, the **following prayer** will get you there if you mean it with all your heart:

*"Lord Jesus, I understand that sin has control of me, and I have been OK with that up to now. **But I want more.** I want to know You and know more about Your love for me. **I know Jesus died because of MY sin and I'm sorry.** But I know He died so I could be forgiven, so I ask you now for that forgiveness. I want to live life as you intended. **I want Jesus to be the Lord of my life, now and forever.** I believe your promises and ask you to allow me to pass from death to life at this very moment. I pray this now in the powerful name of Jesus. Amen"*

If you prayed those words for the first time and meant them in your heart, I can assure you, based on the truth of Scripture, that you've crossed the line. Welcome to the Kingdom of Life! But there's lots more to understand about the Faith God provides.

The Source of Faith

Faith is an IRREVOCABLE GIFT based on hearing and believing. Many people believe faith is just something we already have or can manifest anytime we decide to exercise it. But faith is much more complicated.

The often-used example of faith is that of the child who leaps from the top of the steps into the waiting arms of a mother or father. Yet that kind of faith isn't based on whimsy. Faith like that is based on trust. In fact, the Greek word for "faith" also forms the root for the words "believe" and "trust". Therefore,

> **Belief = Trust = Faith.**

It's no accident that the language in which the New Testament is written is Greek. It is a language of very specific meanings that allows for the expression of linguistic nuances. Like the small child who leaps into space believing a parent will catch her, so are we who TRUST in the saving power of Jesus Christ. We believe. Not because we have some super-power that allows us to have faith in the unknown, but because God has somehow infused our hearts with trust in Him.

God's grace – His "unmerited favor" – is at the heart of our Faith. We believe because He enables us to do so. We trust because He has shown Himself to be trustworthy. **Our faith is rooted in HIM, not in us.** And lest we begin to take some credit for our faith in God and our resulting eternal redemption, Paul reminds us in his letter to the Ephesians:

> *God saved you by his grace when you believed. And **you can't take credit for this**; it is a **gift from God**. Salvation is not a reward for the good things we have done, so none of us can boast about it.   Ephesians 2:8-9 NLT*

Why do any of us ever believe in the promises of a God we cannot see? Because God has mysteriously made Himself known to us, whether we acknowledge that truth or not. In Romans, Paul writes:

> **They know the truth about God because he has made it obvious to them.** *For ever since the world was created, people have seen the earth and sky. Through everything God made, they can clearly see his invisible qualities –* **His eternal power and divine nature***. So, they have no excuse for not knowing God.*
> Romans 1:19-20 NLT

> **Each of us has the truth of God written on our hearts when we are formed.**

We inherently understand "His eternal power". God can do anything He says because He is omnipotent – all powerful. He has a perfect, just, and holy "divine nature" that never varies because He is immutable – unchangeable.

Those qualities have made trusting God – believing His promises – a reasonable thing to do "since the world was created", as Paul said in Romans. Our only hurdle is to acknowledge what is already true about God. And about us. Paul goes a step further in Romans 3:

> *For everyone has sinned; **we all fall short of God's glorious standard**. Yet God, in his grace, freely makes us right in his sight. He did this through Christ Jesus when he freed us from the penalty for our sins. For God presented Jesus as the sacrifice for sin. **People are made right with God when they believe** that Jesus sacrificed his life, shedding his blood.   Romans 3:23-25 NLT*

We can't possibly understand the truths about God and His character without seeing ourselves in the light of His holiness. When that happens, we don't look very good. Sin is ugly, but most of the time we ignore it or excuse it in our lives. Trusting God and believing His promises for our future metamorphosis requires that we acknowledge who we really are before Him. His infusion of faith into our lives is contingent on our humble confession of our sin and need for salvation.

Once we've done that, **belief** becomes **trust**, which grows into **faith** by the power of the Spirit of God.

The Life of Faith

Our salvation through Christ's atoning death on the cross doesn't just get us a ticket to heaven. The Gospel, and our salvation, are about so much more!

Once we understand the beginnings of our faith and the source of our faith, how should we then understand living our lives IN faith?

> **We should be living lives of service because we've been empowered for MINISTRY.**

Empowered by whom? By the Spirit of God. Why does He empower us? Because the work of Kingdom-building is an ongoing process! There is much work to be done:

> *(Jesus) said to his disciples, "The harvest is great, but the workers are few. So, pray to the Lord who is in charge of the harvest; ask him to **send more workers** into his fields."*
> *Matthew 9:37-38 NLT*

More workers. That would be you and me. We have been summoned to a life of service to the Master of our Salvation. A life of faith isn't about deciding how we choose to live. It is a life spent in obedient service to the Giver of Life. How do we fulfill our roles as Kingdom builders?

As Peter writes in the following text, when we speak or serve using God's empowering gifts, we are doing it with His voice and His energy and His strength!

> *God has given each of you a gift from his great variety of spiritual gifts. Use them well to serve one another.* **Do you have the gift of speaking?** *Then speak as though God himself were speaking through you.* **Do you have the gift of helping others?** *Do it with all the strength and energy that God supplies.* **Then everything you do will bring glory to God through Jesus Christ.**
> *1 Peter 4:10-11 NLT*

Ask yourself, "Does *empowered* mean the power comes from inside you or outside of you?" Just as our Faith comes from God, so does the power for ministry. You may have the ability to use your voice, as Peter says, to help build the Kingdom of God – to teach or preach or counsel. Or you may be less vocal but use your hands and feet in the service of others in so many different ways. But EVERY believer who ministers through the power of the Holy Spirit does it with a heart filled with humility and gratitude for what Jesus has done.

We should be living ABUNDANTLY here and now.

When we receive the gift of salvation, we step from life that is the "best we can do" into an existence that will last for eternity. We don't have to wait until we get to heaven to enjoy eternal life. We have already passed from death to life. What are you waiting for?

Jesus said, "*I have come that they may have life, and that they may have it **more abundantly**.*" *John 10:10*

Most of us think of eternal life as something we inherit when we die. We've got THIS life and then the NEXT life. But when we pass from death to life, we enter an existence that never ends – an **eternal** life. How do we know what that looks like? Jesus gave us a clear picture about what life is like in His realm:

> "*God blesses those who are poor and **realize their need for him**…God blesses those who **mourn**…God blesses those who are **humble**…God blesses those who **hunger and thirst for justice**…God blesses those who are **merciful**…God blesses those whose **hearts are pure**…God blesses those who **work for peace**…God blesses those who are **persecuted for doing right**…God blesses you when people mock you and persecute you and lie about you and say all sorts of evil things against you **because you are my followers**….*" *Matthew 5:3-11 NLT*

What Jesus said in those few verses He expanded on in the rest of the Sermon on the Mount in *Matthew 5-7*. It might not all sound rosy, but when you read over the list again, it sounds like Jesus, doesn't it? He came so we would know what the Kingdom looks like. He came so we would know what God is like. So if we are to spend eternity with Him, doesn't it make sense that we'd begin to live now like we'll live then?

And those less-than-pleasant side effects of living for Jesus NOW, like being persecuted and mocked and lied about? He took care of that once we leave this earthly existence:

> "Look, God's home is now among his people! He will live with them, and they will be his people. God himself will be with them. **He will wipe every tear** from their eyes, and there will be **no more death or sorrow or crying or pain**. All these things are gone forever."
> Revelation 21:3-4 NLT

God knows something about life that we don't. He knows that living for Him is better than living for ourselves, no matter what we may have to tolerate. Because the payoff is worth it. After all, we can't live FOR Jesus if we aren't trying to live LIKE Jesus.

We should be living as the IMAGE-BEARERS of GOD in the world.

When people saw Jesus, they saw God. That was the plan all along for Jesus. But it was also God's plan all for me and you. **We were created to showcase the character of God**. That fact is likely either very encouraging or very intimidating – or both. But it IS very true:

> *Then God said, "Let us make human beings **in Our image**, to be like Us… So, God created human beings in his own image. In the image of God, He created them; male and female He created them.   Genesis 1:26-27 NLT*

When you look in the mirror, do you see the Image-Bearer of God? What do you think when you realize that God's reputation in the world is related to how you and I live since we call ourselves followers of Jesus? It's always difficult to think in the abstract about what it means to be the Image-Bearer of God. But the writer of *Hebrews* has given us a description of Jesus to help us:

> *The Son radiates God's own glory and expresses the very character of God... Hebrews 1:3a NLT*

Just as the moon only reflects the brightness of the sun, we should, like Jesus, reflect the glory of God. HIS character should be OUR character. Everything we do should draw attention to the God who created us in His image. Which makes this passage from Jesus' Sermon on the Mount make even more sense:

> *"You are the light of the world – like a city on a hilltop that cannot be hidden. No one lights a lamp and then puts it under a basket. Instead, a lamp is placed on a stand, where it gives light*

to everyone in the house. In the same way, **let your good deeds shine** *out for all to see,* **so that everyone will praise your heavenly Father.** Matthew 5:14-16 NLT

When you live a life of faith, others should notice. They should see the "good deeds" you do and "praise your heavenly father". Remember – when people saw Jesus, they saw God. YOUR life of faith will cause them to do the same.

We should be living in WAYS WE NEVER ANTICIPATED.

IF we trust the Spirit of God to direct us, He will take us places we don't expect. We all have our preconceived plans about what life should be like, but **what if God wants to surprise you?** Would you rather just live out the life you currently anticipate or allow the Spirit of God to take you where you never imagined you would go?

On the last night He was alive, Jesus shared the following words with His closest disciples:

> *"I tell you the truth, anyone who believes in me will do the same works I have done,* **and even greater works***, because I am going to be with the Father.* John 14:12 NLT

Wouldn't you like to have led a group discussion with the Twelve after dinner that night to see what they thought Jesus meant? They had watched Jesus raise the dead, feed thousands with a little boy's lunch, and calm the wind and sea. Yet He was telling them they would do even "**greater works** than these". What in the world could He be talking about?

While Jesus commanded the physical universe around Him (He did make it, after all), I believe Jesus was promising the disciples that their commission to take the Gospel to the world would be an even "greater work". Jesus spoke these words of encouragement when He shared what we term the "Great Commission" with His disciples:

> *Jesus came and told his disciples, "I have been given all authority in heaven and on earth. Therefore, go and **make disciples of all the nations**, baptizing them in the name of the Father and the Son and the Holy Spirit. Teach these new disciples to obey all the commands I have given you. And be sure of this: **I am with you always, even to the end of the age**."*
> *Matthew 28:19-20 NLT*

Can we re-convene that discussion group now? Make disciples of ALL nations. Don't just reach the Jews; not just all of Israel. In fact, if you reach the whole Roman empire with the promise of salvation through Jesus Christ you will have failed! The

WHOLE WORLD is your target. I doubt even Peter, James, and John expected that when they signed up.

If you can empathize with what they were feeling, that's good. Because we, as followers of our Lord, Jesus Christ, have been given the same kind of responsibility:

> **God has given us this task of reconciling people to him**...*So we are Christ's ambassadors;* **God is making his appeal through us**. *We speak for Christ when we plead, "Come back to God!"*
> 2 Corinthians 5:18,20

"Wait a minute! I didn't realize living this Life of Faith would be so challenging!" If that thought just ran through your mind, I'd say you're perfectly normal. We didn't realize what was expected of us. Neither did the first disciples when they responded to Jesus' call to "Follow Me". Nor do we realize just what we're capable of when we live a life of faith.

Paul worked hard to fulfill his responsibility to his Lord, and he encouraged his readers to do the same with this amazing promise from God:

> *Now all glory to God, who is able, through his mighty power at work* **within us**, *to accomplish* **infinitely more** *than we might ask or think.*
> *Ephesians 3:20*

27

What does that look like in your life? I have no idea, but God certainly is up to the task. Where will God take you if you are willing to be used by Him? I have no idea, but God knows the way wherever it might be. The question really is, "Are you willing to be used in ways you never anticipated by the God in Whom you've placed your trust?"

Finally, write this question on a 3x5 card and put it on the refrigerator or make it your screen saver: **"If you could do ANYTHING for God in the next five years with no fear of failure or finances, what would it be?"** Just don't forget that God said He can do "infinitely more than we might ask or think", so get ready for what comes next.

> **We should be living so we IDENTIFY people and projects to INVEST in for eternal results.**

Identify and Invest. That sounds like "Time" and "Money". Most of us are pretty possessive of both, yet not a single breath we take or dollar we make are apart from the goodness of God. Our lives of faith are to be spent in gratitude for the great price Jesus paid to redeem us. We can't cling to either our time or money when they can make an eternal difference. Our challenge is to figure out **where and in whom we should dedicate our time and wealth.**

Regarding our material wealth, Jesus had lots to say, including these words:

> *"**Don't store up treasures here on earth**, where moths eat them and rust destroys them, and where thieves break in and steal. **Store your treasures in heaven**... Wherever your treasure is, there the desires of your heart will also be.   Matthew 6:19-21 NLT*

Since Jesus spent more time talking about money than about heaven or hell, we'll be looking more at the issue in later chapters. Suffice it to say that HAVING money has nothing to do with righteousness. USING wealth in view of eternity has everything to do with righteousness:

> *And if you are untrustworthy about **worldly wealth**, who will trust you with the **true riches** of heaven?   Luke 16:11 NLT*

Passages like the Great Commission (*Matthew 28:18-20*) challenge us to "make disciples". That can be a real test, can't it? Make a quick list in your mind of all those in whom you've invested your life so they might grow in their faith. Did you think of any names? I said it can be a challenge. However, the challenge is usually in us, not in the resistance of the one to be discipled. Paul wrote to his disciple, Timothy, this encouragement:

You have heard me teach things that have been confirmed by many reliable witnesses. **Now teach these truths to other trustworthy people who will be able to pass them on to others.** *2 Timothy 2:2*

Take note of the four generations of disciples in the passage: Paul, who had been teaching Timothy; Timothy, who should be teaching what he learned to "trustworthy people"; and the "others" who would receive the teaching from those "trustworthy" folks in whom Timothy had invested himself.

We get eternal results when we invest our wealth and time in causes and people who can multiply our efforts. Sure, we should choose carefully, since most of us are short on both time and money. But 4th Quarter life is all about leaving a Legacy. I can think of no greater legacy than to leave an inheritance in the hearts of those in whom we invest ourselves and our wealth.

Can you imagine being able to write words like those of Paul as you finish your life of faith:

> *The only letter of recommendation we need is you yourselves.* **Your lives are a letter written in our hearts**; *everyone can read it and recognize our good work among you. Clearly,* **you are a letter from Christ showing the result of our ministry among you**. *This*

"letter" is written not with pen and ink, but with the Spirit of the living God. It is carved not on tablets of stone, but on human hearts.
2 Corinthians 3:2-3

Never stop learning about, and growing in, your Faith. Our faith may be simple enough for a child to understand, but there is little that is simple about living it. Don't stop. Finish strong for Christ.

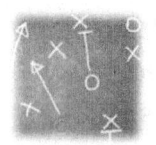

Strategy #2 – Commit to continually honor God through your MINISTRY.

Ministry, for the believer, should be the natural outflow of a life of Faith. But life gets busy and there are other time demands our culture tries to place on us. What's left? Often, we "do" ministry in small bits when we can work it into our schedule. But Paul had his priorities right when he shared:

> "...my life is worth nothing to me **unless I use it for finishing the work assigned me by the Lord Jesus** – the work of telling others the Good News about the wonderful grace of God." Acts 20:24 NLT

Have you stopped to consider that the God who formed you – the God who sacrificed for your salvation – has also **assigned a work of ministry specifically for you**? Paul knew what work God had called him to. Do you?

The Nature of Ministry

Before we go further, it would be helpful to define **Ministry**. Before you read more, think about how YOU would define it.

> *Wikipedia says*: "In Christianity, **ministry** is an activity carried out by Christians to express or spread their faith, the prototype being the Great Commission."

> *The Encyclopedia of Christianity* defines **ministry** as "carrying forth Christ's mission in the world", indicating that it is "conferred on each Christian in baptism."

Both definitions seem to exclude the idea that Ministry is both **required and assigned by God**. And neither really speaks much about the **specificity** of ministry, only speaking about it in general terms like "fulfilling the Great Commission". Yet according to Scripture, ministry is **expected, personal, and specific**.

From where does the word "Ministry" derive? Two Greek words with the same origin explain more about what ministry should mean for us. *Διάκονος (diakonos)* means "One who executes the commands of another; a servant or minister." *Διακονία (diakonia)* simply means "Ministry or ministering or serving."

It should be clear then that **ministry involves serving**. But serving whom? Jesus' words in response to a question will help us understand:

> *"Teacher, which is the **most important commandment** in the law of Moses?"*
> *Jesus replied, "'You must love the Lord your God with all your heart, all your soul, and all*

33

> your mind.' **This is the first and greatest commandment. A second is equally important:** *'Love your neighbor as yourself.'* Matthew 22:36-39

Our ministry, or service, is a "both/and". We are to love God with every part of our being, and if we do that, we will love those around us as well. This section of Scripture is referred to as the "Great Commandment" (not to be confused with the Great Commission). In it, Jesus summarizes what the nature of our lives should be as people of faith. Our dedicated service to God results in our dedicated service to others. "Both/and".

Ministry is offered in gratitude to God, but the direct beneficiaries of our service are those around us. Particularly those who have not heard the Good News, that Jesus gave His life to redeem those who are irrevocably lost without His grace.

If we revisit Paul's words to the elders from Ephesus in *Acts 20*, we discover not only his commitment to his ministry, but his understanding of WHAT that ministry entails:

> "...*my life is worth nothing to me unless I use it for finishing the work assigned me by the Lord Jesus –* **the work of telling others the Good News about the wonderful grace of God.**" Acts 20:24 NLT

Paul's ministry involved taking the Good News about Jesus to people who otherwise might never hear it. These weren't "religious" people but were, in fact, downright pagan. Paul was comfortable teaching others about God in the context of his Jewish upbringing. But God moved him outside his comfort zone (and that of every other Jewish Bible teacher of his day) to SERVE others by bringing them the Good News. Paul's job in the Body of Christ was to MINISTER the word of God to those who would become the people of God. And he did it well:

> *I have done the Lord's work humbly and with many tears. I have endured the trials that came to me from the plots of the Jews.* **I never shrank back from telling you what you needed to hear**, *either publicly or in your homes. I have had* **one message** *for Jews and Greeks alike –* **the necessity of repenting from sin and turning to God, and of having faith in our Lord Jesus.** Acts 20:19-21 NLT

Paul also clearly understood the **source** of his power to do ministry.

Based on our faith and the indwelling Holy Spirit, we have each been EMPOWERED for ministry.

Since we spent some time talking about empowerment in our discussion of living a life of faith, let's focus on the purpose for empowerment. Paul wrote to Timothy:

> *I thank Christ Jesus our Lord,* **who has given me strength** *to do his work. He considered me trustworthy and appointed me to serve him….*
> 1 Timothy 1:12 NLT

The word translated "given…strength" is translated "empowered" in other versions and is derived from the Greek word **δύναμις** *(dunamis)* from which we get our words "dynamite" and "dynamo". The implication is that there is tremendous power and strength derived directly from the Holy Spirit of God. It is that strength and power that drives our ministry, whatever it is.

The Gifts for Ministry

The apostle Paul understood that his power for ministry came from outside himself – it was a gift from the Holy Spirit. But Paul was also gifted with an **ability** to fulfill the calling of God in his life. He had discovered that his role in the kingdom-building process to which each member of the Church is commissioned was *"telling others the Good News about the wonderful grace of God" (Acts 20:24).* Did Paul already possess all the skill and insight to fulfill his role in the Church? He was a gifted teacher and he had the right pedigree to do the job. But listen to what Paul says about his "human" abilities:

> We rely on what Christ Jesus has done for us. **We put no confidence in human effort,** though I could have confidence in my own effort if anyone could. Indeed, if others have reason for confidence in their own efforts, I have even more!   Philippians 3:3-4

Paul was reminding us that our human effort will produce human results. If we want to see God do the amazing things He promised to do in *Ephesians 3:20*, we need to **let Him do it through us**!

> Now all glory to God, who is able, **through his mighty power** at work **within us**, to accomplish **infinitely more** than we might ask or think.   Ephesians 3:20 NLT

Ministry is not based on human effort.

> **Effective ministry is a result of the redeemed of Christ using the SUPERNATURAL RESOURCES of the Holy Spirit to bring glory to God the Father.**

Now that we've established that God has empowered us and intends us to use HIS power in our service and ministry, how DO we know what ministry God has assigned to us? We start by serving and observing how God blesses what we do. If you aren't sure whether you're called to be a 21st century Paul or the next Billy Graham, try to **serve in any capacity** which might present itself. Then evaluate your fruitfulness (and sanity) and determine whether that role is a possibility or not.

Consider some of the following passages as you pray for understanding:

> ***God has given each of you a gift*** *from his great variety of spiritual gifts. Use them well to serve one another. Do you have the gift of* ***speaking****? Then speak as though God himself were speaking through you. Do you have the gift of* ***helping*** *others? Do it with all the strength and energy that God supplies. Then everything you do will bring glory to God through Jesus Christ.   1 Peter 4:10-11 NLT*

God gifts **each** of us a gift which might be a <u>speaking gift</u> or a <u>helping/serving gift</u>. Most people have an immediate idea into which category they fit.

> **This "gift" which is given to us by the indwelling Holy Spirit is designed to fit our personality and skill set.**

Imagine you are purchasing a gift for someone. How do you decide what to give? You consider what they like and what they don't like. You take into account their personality and what they already possess. Do you think the Holy Spirit is at least as careful about gift-giving as you are? Therefore, trust that whichever spiritual gift with which you've been entrusted is perfect for you.

Paul gets even more specific than Peter when he teaches us about the spiritual gifts available in the Holy Spirit's arsenal:

> *In his grace, God has given us different gifts for doing certain things well. So, if God has given you the ability to **prophesy**, speak out with as much faith as God has given you. If your gift is **serving** others, serve them well. If you are a **teacher**, teach well. If your gift is to **encourage** others, be encouraging. If it is **giving**, give generously. If God has given you **leadership** ability, take the responsibility seriously. And if you have a gift for showing **kindness** (mercy) to others, do it gladly.*
> Romans 12:6-8 NLT

Paul lists seven gifts that the Holy Spirit provides, **each of which Jesus perfectly modeled** for our ministries. Because Jesus was completely filled by the Holy Spirit, and because everything He did was perfectly submitted to the will of the Father, we can be sure these gifts are available to us. In fact, when the Church ministers using these gifts, God's plan is that those who have never had a personal encounter with

Jesus see Him in our Ministry and are drawn to Him. It's critical to understand that **any gift you have is never intended to draw attention to you**, but only to glorify Christ and empower you to do Kingdom work.

Comparing Paul's list to Peter's, you'll see that each of the gifts mentioned by Paul fits nicely into the two broader categories cited by Peter. The "speaking gifts" include prophecy, teaching, and encouragement or exhortation; and the "helping or serving gifts" include service, leadership, giving, and kindness or mercy. God's Word is consistent when His messengers are faithful!

The wonderful thing about these gifts listed by Paul is that **while ONE is the primary gift that empowers your ministry, as you grow in faith and following after Christ, you'll begin to exhibit characteristics of ALL the gifts.** That's a part of what "being conformed to the Image of Christ" is all about. We serve side-by-side with others in the Body of Christ and we learn what the gifts look like in action. The more we see the Church reflect the nature of Jesus through its ministry, the better we can emulate those gifts in our own lives and service, even if they aren't our primary gift.

Ask yourself, "Which of the seven gifts mentioned by Paul most fits me, as God made me?" When you answer that question, you are well on the way to discovery. However, any gift you may possess that is ignored or neglected will cause you to be confused about what God is doing in and through you. You can't know HOW God can use you unless you do something!

The Rewards of Ministry

Our discussion so far has been centered on what God is doing in us and through us as we serve Him. But how does engaging in ministry by being obedient to the calling and gifting of God affect US?

> **Our Ministry allows us to FULFILL OUR CALLING in Christ.**

We've been called to serve and glorify God as a part of being united together as the Body of Christ. Our Ministry allows us to live up to that calling.

> *But you are not like that, for you are a **chosen people**. You are **royal priests, a holy nation**, God's very own possession. As a result, you can show others the goodness of God, for he called you out of the darkness into his wonderful light.   1 Peter 2:9 NLT*

Are you amazed that God, in His infinite wisdom, determined that YOU are to be His "very own possession"? He is working through you and there is no Plan B. Your service for Christ, whatever your ministry and giftedness might be, is a holy calling. Peter told us this in his second letter:

> *So, dear brothers and sisters, work hard to prove that you really are among those God has **called and chosen**.* 2 Peter 1:10 NLT

God took all the initiative in making us His. What we do in ministry allows us to fulfill our calling and validate His love.

Our Ministry UNITES US TOGETHER as one Body in Christ.

Because each of us is just a **part** of what God is doing, we must be **united** in our purpose and service so we can collectively fulfill ALL the purposes of God. We are so much stronger together than we are individually:

> *Just as our bodies have many parts and each part has a special function, **so it is with Christ's body**. We are many parts of one body, and **we all belong to each other**.* Romans 12:4-5 NLT

No doubt you've heard the old adage from a coach at some point, "There's no "I" in TEAM." Well, there's no "I" in CHURCH either. We focus too much on those few who are very gifted speakers in the Church, some of whom enjoy rock-star fame. But who takes care of the parking lots at their churches? Who watches babies in their church nurseries? And who provides the tithes and offerings to support their preaching and book writing and radio programming?

When the Church functions as it **should**, EVERY part has a function. EACH of us is doing ministry so that the Body of Christ reveals the Person of Christ to the world. No one has ever had all the gifts like Jesus. But He gave all the gifts to His Church collectively. Do your part! Otherwise, the world can't see a true picture of the One who came to save them.

> **Our ministry** *(and the results we see)* **gives us ASSURANCE that we belong to Christ and BRINGS GLORY TO GOD.**

If our chief purpose as believers is to glorify God in all we do, Ministry is a key component in that effort. When we see God blessing our work in Ministry, we can be certain we belong to Him.

> *When you produce much fruit, you are my* **true disciples**. *This brings great* **glory** *to my Father.* John 15:8 NLT

Jesus spent much of His time reminding the disciples that the key to their success would be determined by whether or not they stayed "plugged in" to the power of God. Their fruitfulness, He said, would come only if they continued to "abide in Him". But His teaching wasn't just for the purpose of producing "fruit". More happens when we serve God than just the yield at harvest. We show ourselves to be HIS, and God is glorified. It's not all about results. It's about our connection with the Father, Son, and Holy Spirit.

When we minister in the power of the Spirit, we get feedback:

> For **His Spirit joins with our spirit to affirm** that we are God's children.   Romans 8:16 NLT

Why do Christians sometimes go through periods of DOUBTING THEIR SALVATION experience?

Likely because they have DAMAGED THEIR CONNECTION with God.

Perhaps sin has taken hold and they are reminded by Satan that they are unworthy to be called God's own? Aren't we all? But when we are struggling with sin in our lives, we start to believe the Father of Lies.

More commonly, we doubt our connection to God because we lack the feedback from the Spirit. Our connection with God has "corroded" due to lack of use. When we serve God through ministry, we draw power from Him to complete our service. He, in turn, reminds us that we are "God's children".

All 4th Quarter adults deal with fatigue and disillusionment and insecurity at some point. You are not alone if you've been there or are languishing there now. When we serve Christ in our area of Ministry it helps combat each of those weak spots because we know we're a part of **something bigger than ourselves** that is making an eternal difference!

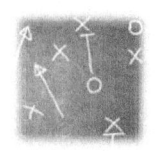

Strategy #3 – Live as a careful STEWARD of all God provides.

We live as Followers of Christ in a world that functions in ways that undermine Biblical guidelines. We are bombarded by advertisements reminding us to "have it OUR way"; that we need things we could certainly do without; and that unless we dress the right way or drive the right car, we're never going to make it in life! How do we decide how to handle the wealth we're blessed with and who sets the priorities for our spending and saving? The short answer is: GOD. The decision to be a careful steward is critical to honoring God in the area of finance.

How does the World view wealth?

- The world equates wealth with success and happiness.
- The world says, "Get as much as you can, can all you get, and sit on the can!"

But God's wisdom is different from the wisdom of the world. Solomon, who was blessed with Godly wisdom said this about money:

> **Those who love money will never have enough.** *How meaningless to think that wealth brings true happiness!* **The more you have, the more people come to help you spend it.**

So, what good is wealth – except perhaps to watch it slip through your fingers!
Ecclesiastes 5:10-11 NLT

Most of us aren't wealthy and probably wonder what really rich people do with all their money. Some people who have a lot of money have made it by taking advantage of others; others were simply born with the proverbial "silver spoon" in their mouths. The vast majority of Christians have to live life on the same amount of money as their non-Christian friends and neighbors. Why then should we live **differently**?

The Purpose of Money

Everything that's critical to know in life is contained in the pages of Scripture, and God certainly has a purpose in providing material goods to people. Money is our means of paying for labor and goods, so it is vital to function in our society. Humans have always found a way to trade something for what they want. Money, in our culture, makes exchange easier than trading chickens for gasoline. We place a value on an item and exchange it for some amount of money equal in value to the item. If this is a "worldly" system of commerce, why does Scripture seem to imply money has spiritual significance?

More than 2,300 verses in the Bible have to do with money and possessions, and 30% of the parables

Jesus told were about money. That makes it important!

> **God provides money because we need to exchange it for the BASIC NECESSITIES of life.**

God knows we have needs. Food and clothing for starters. Most of us expect housing and a car that runs! What does the Bible say about basics?

> *Yet true godliness with contentment is itself great wealth. After all, we brought nothing with us when we came into the world, and we can't take anything with us when we leave it. So, **if we have enough food and clothing**, let us be content.   1 Timothy 6:6-8 NLT*

Most of us would balk at that statement. Just food and clothing? Maybe Paul got the idea from Jesus' teaching?

> *"So, don't worry about these things, saying, 'What will we **eat**? What will we **drink**? What will we **wear**?' These things **dominate the thoughts of unbelievers**, but your heavenly Father already knows all your needs. Matthew 6:31-32 NLT*

There it is again! Food and clothing are obvious necessities. We DO need to dress and eat. But what else? We've come to expect more, haven't we? God knows we need the basics and He promises to provide them.

Take this one-question quiz on the first purpose of money: **"Has God provided the basic necessities for your life, including food, clothing, shelter, and even transportation (even if you have to ride the bus)?"** Maybe this would be a good time to express your gratitude to God for His faithfulness in meeting your needs?

But if money is intended to supply only OUR basic necessities, what are we supposed to do with all the EXTRA money we have?

> **God provides money so we can be the agent through whom He MEETS THE NEEDS OF OTHERS.**

Everyone has needs. Not only you, but your neighbor as well. That nice lady that scans your groceries may have just lost her husband. What will she do now to make ends meet? You know that family of five that lives down your street? The father just lost his job. How will they make ends meet? The answer to both questions might be that God will use YOU.

God promises He will meet all our needs, but He doesn't say HOW. Sometimes our needs might have to be met through the generosity of others. Oh, how embarrassing! Does God see it that way?

> Right now, **you have plenty and can help those who are in need. Later, they will have plenty and can share with you** when you need it.   2 Corinthians 8:14 NLT

An attitude of self-reliance is prideful.

God wants us to know that it is HE who provides for our needs. We are not sufficient in and of ourselves. Jesus reminded the disciples to pray for their "daily bread". Does that idea seem alien to you?

God provided the Israelites with manna every day in the desert. There, they were completely dependent on Him. Just to be sure they understood their dependence on Him, God had Moses warn them before He allowed them to pass into the Promised Land flowing with great wealth:

> He (God) did all this so you would never say to yourself, '**I have achieved this wealth with my own strength and energy.**' Remember the Lord your God. **He is the one who gives you power to be successful**....
> Deuteronomy 8:17-18 NLT

Why does God allow some to have needs and others to have plenty? To remind both that **He is the One**

who provides. If we truly grasp that God is our supplier, it makes sharing what He gives us much easier:

> And God will generously provide all you need. Then **you will always have everything you need, and plenty left over to share with others.** As the Scriptures say, "They share freely and give generously to the poor. Their good deeds will be remembered forever."
> 2 Corinthians 9:8-9 NLT

The main question you may ask yourself is, **"Do I wish to be the person through whom God supplies the needs of others and be blessed for doing it?"**

God provides money to be INVESTED FOR KINGDOM PURPOSES.

Consider all the costs associated with taking the Gospel of Jesus Christ to the whole world. Printing costs, transportation costs, lodging costs, providing food for the hungry, and caring for those in deep need, like widows and orphans. Salary support for pastors and missionaries, medical costs to support staff, money to dig clean wells, money to buy building materials for necessary projects, money to purchase mosquito netting, and lots of money to provide medicine to the indigent. I could obviously go on…and on.

When Jesus sent out the first large group of disciples to share the Gospel, He told them this:

> **Don't take any money with you**, nor a traveler's bag, nor an extra pair of sandals. And don't stop to greet anyone on the road. Whenever you enter someone's home, first say, "May God's peace be on this house." If those who live there are peaceful, the blessing will stand; if they are not, the blessing will return to you. Don't move around from home to home. Stay in one place, eating and drinking what they provide. Don't hesitate to accept hospitality, because **those who work deserve their pay.** Luke 10:4-7 NLT

Can you imagine missionaries or church planters heading out without being "fully-funded"? That's not the way we do it now. But Jesus wanted the disciples to know that He was going ahead of them through the power of the Holy Spirit and would meet their basic needs. Jesus expected there to be a willingness among those who were spiritually-minded to give to support those who do God's work in the world.

Most church planting and mission organizations would never risk sending their folks out without knowing they would be taken care of in the field. Those same organizations could be accused of lacking the faith of the early disciples. But remember it was Jesus who sent them out that way INTENTIONALLY. **Accepting**

God's provision is an act of faith and gratitude. Once our basic necessities are met, what we do next speaks volumes about our priorities.

No discussion of money and the kingdom could possibly be complete without these words from Jesus:

> Don't **store up** treasures here on earth, where moths eat them and rust destroys them, and where thieves break in and steal. **Store your treasures in heaven**, where moths and rust cannot destroy, and thieves do not break in and steal. **Wherever your treasure is, there the desires of your heart will also be**.
> Matthew 6:19-21 NLT

It seems the Biblical imperative regarding wealth is that it should be used to provide for one's own needs, **then** the needs of others, and **then** used for kingdom-building, NOT accumulating. Scripture is clear that hard work and diligence will result in some measure of prosperity. But nowhere in the Bible does it teach that we should be working to accumulate wealth for our own "security".

As followers of Jesus and servants of God, we must find our security in His provision, not in our savings.

Consider that a dollar invested in a savings account gains interest; a dollar invested in a Kingdom project has the potential to help others gain eternity.

The Principle of Stewardship

For Christians, a giant step in developing our faith is to understand and accept the principle of Stewardship. Let's begin this discussion with a general definition:

> **STEWARDSHIP: A personal commitment by one party to overseeing assets which are owned by another.**

That sounds kind of like a lawyer put the definition together, but it makes God's intention for us clear. We, as God's creation, are agreeing to oversee assets which belong to someone else – GOD. Don't be surprised by the arrangement. God established the principle of stewardship from the very beginning:

> *The Lord God placed the man in the Garden of Eden **to tend and watch over it.***
> *Genesis 2:15 NLT*

Did Adam own the garden? No. Did Adam own anything? No. As humans have inhabited the Earth for millennia, they have gradually gotten the idea that they OWN things. Kings have claimed lands through conquest. Explorers have claimed lands already occupied by others. No doubt, your home is located on land once occupied by someone else in history, but now you claim ownership of that particular plot of ground. You own your clothes. You own your bank account. What else do you think you "own"?

Job understood the principle of stewardship and had a healthy understanding about how God's provision to us works:

> *He said, "I came naked from my mother's womb, and I will be naked when I leave.* ***The Lord gave me what I had****, and the Lord has taken it away. Praise the name of the Lord!"   Job 1:21 NLT*

From Adam to Job, from Moses to Jesus, from YOU to your heirs, **no one really owns anything**. We are just stewards of all that God provides. To be certain I'm being as clear as I can be, stewardship is not the same as ownership.

Stewardship ≠ Ownership

If we're still on the same page regarding stewardship, what else does the Bible say about it?

> *The earth is the Lord's, and* ***everything in it****. The world and all its people* ***belong to him****. Psalm 24:1 NLT*

55

God says "everything" and "all" belong to Him. That should be pretty clear, so here's another:

> *He (God) did all this so you would never say to yourself, '**I have achieved this wealth with my own strength and energy**.' Remember the Lord your God. **He is the one who gives** you power to be successful....*
> *Deuteronomy 8:17-18 NLT*

What, then, does the Bible add to our definition of Stewardship?

BIBLICAL STEWARDSHIP
involves total commitment of myself and my possessions to God's service, knowing that since HE owns everything,
I DON'T HAVE ANY RIGHTS OF CONTROL
over my property or my life.

Why do you think there's a difference between how the world views wealth and how the Bible views it? Because the Bible shows us the **truth about God** and His creation and His provision, **while the world creates its own system of belief.** As a faithful follower of Christ, don't expect that the world will see things like you do. Assuming you see the difference, pause and ask yourself this question:

Which view of money have you more closely followed up to this point in your life, the world's or God's?

Let's summarize some of the principles taught in the pages of Scripture about wealth and Stewardship:

- Whatever I have belongs to God, **including all my money**. Everything. All of it. Ask yourself, "If that is true, how will that impact how I handle money in the future?

- God provides for me and my family and **grants me a surplus so I can be His agent** of provision in the lives of others. We usually focus on the first part and neglect the last part of that statement. Have you handled your finances in a way that acknowledges that you see yourself as an agent of God to provide for the basic necessities of others?

- If I don't have a surplus and I haven't been using what God has provided to meet the needs of others, **WHY would I expect God to give me more**? Expecting God to bless us financially only for our own benefit is selfish. If you have not been using the abundance God has provided according to His plan, how do you intend to change?

  *To **those who use well what they are given, even more will be given**, and they will have an abundance. But from those who do nothing,* even what little they have will be taken away.   Matthew 25:29 NLT

Blessed are those who are generous, because they feed the poor.
Proverbs 22:9 NLT

Jesus taught us:

*And if you are untrustworthy about worldly wealth, who will trust you with the **true riches** of heaven? And if you are not faithful with other people's things, why should you be trusted with things of your own? "No one can serve two masters. For you will hate one and love the other; you will be devoted to one and despise the other. **You cannot serve God and be enslaved to money.***   Luke 16:11-13 NLT

Why does Scripture speak so much about money? Look at our world. What is the root cause of many of the world's problems? Money, and the quest for it. Whether we focus on the drug trade or human trafficking; white collar crime or insurance fraud; the culprit is the same – Money.

Marital problems primarily associated with "money issues" cause more than 1 in 5 divorces in this country![1] Spending more than we make and

---

[1] https://institutedfa.com/Leading-Causes-Divorce/

borrowing to make up the difference is a terrible problem in America. Young college students who attend school on someone else's dime to major in a field that will never get them a competitive job are disillusioned at best, and likely saddled with a debt that many may never repay.

Is that what God expects of His children?

> **God wants us to live differently than the world, so the world sees us differently!**

King David, who reigned over some mayhem in his own day, had this to say regarding God's own people:

> *Once I was young, and now I am old. Yet **I have never seen the godly abandoned or their children begging for bread.***
> *Psalm 37:25 NLT*

David's words shouldn't be seen as a promise from God for every Believer but should be understood as the likely outcome **only** for those who are following godly principles. God is ALWAYS faithful to us when we follow His principles.

If you've made it this far, you already have an opinion about whether you've been faithful to God in the area of finances and stewardship. What if you haven't handled your finances like you think you should have?

What if your life doesn't look like what Scripture portrays?

How can you get back on track?

- ✓ Acknowledge your **Stewardship**, not Ownership of all you possess. You have to start somewhere.

- ✓ Recognize that you are **accountable** to God for how you handle His resources. *(Matthew 25:14-30)*. Accountability is scary, but you **are** accountable to God because you are his servant and steward.

- ✓ Develop financial habits that include **budgeting, saving, and generosity.**

  The wise have wealth and luxury, but fools spend whatever they get.   Proverbs 21:20 NLT

  If you think you should be able to spend "your" money as you see fit, go back and study the 1st point again. **Do you currently use some kind of budget, savings, and giving strategy?**

How about one more GIANT step in the process of getting your practice of stewardship back on track?

- ✓ **Start giving** out of **devotion** to God, <u>regardless of your perceived ability to do so.</u>

  While Jesus was in the Temple, he watched the rich people dropping their gifts in the collection box. Then a poor widow came by *and dropped in two small coins. "I tell you the truth," Jesus said, "this poor widow has given more than all the rest of them. For they have given a tiny part of their surplus, but **she, poor as she is, has given everything she has**." Luke 21:1-4 NLT*

If giving demonstrates our love for God, what does it mean if we DO NOT give?

The Power of Giving

Most pastors avoid preaching sermons related to giving in their churches to avoid the criticism that might follow. Their efforts to encourage giving and discuss money-related issues, though certainly Biblical and helpful to those who are really seeking after God, are sometimes met with criticisms similar to this: *"That pastor has stopped preaching and now has gone to meddling!"*

Preaching about money and giving has been perverted by some money-hungry pastors (I'm reluctant to use the word "pastor" for them, but anything else I call them would be decidedly less kind). As a result, many churches go years without hearing an honest message about the Biblical pattern for giving.

I could write a whole book just about the topic of giving, so I'll try to be brief and make only the necessary points so we can be obedient to God's Word.

> **Giving is an act of honoring another.**

Whether the gift is for a birthday or anniversary, the intent is to honor the recipient. In the case of God, we refer to our honor as "worship". The word worship is a shortened version of the Old English word "woerthship" (worth-ship), showing that God is worthy of our honor. One means to honor God is **through our giving** to support Kingdom needs.

What are the general principles of Giving?

- Our gifts should be given **cheerfully and willingly.** Many congregations have even stopped passing an offering plate so that no one feels "required" to give. Unless a gift is given willingly, there is no worship involved.

  *You must each decide in your heart how much to give. And **don't give reluctantly** or in response to pressure. "For God loves a person who gives **cheerfully.**" 2 Corinthians 9:7 NLT*

- What we give should just be **between us and God.** Prideful giving is intended to draw attention to the giver, not honor the recipient.

While not every gift might be able to be given anonymously, there are ways to give without drawing attention to ourselves. (One of those options is to use a Donor-Advised Fund and will be discussed in a later chapter.)

But when you give to someone in need, don't let your left hand know what your right hand is doing. **Give your gifts in private**, *and your Father, who sees everything, will reward you.*
Matthew 6:3-4 NLT

- Our giving should be **to those in need but with an eternal mindset**. Though people have earthly needs, our focus in all we do must be on **heaven**. There is no joy like realizing your gift has been in response to a need that has been lifted to God in prayer by the recipient.

"Sell your possessions and give to those in need. This will store up treasure for you in heaven! And **the purses of heaven never get old or develop holes**. *Your treasure will be safe; no thief can steal it and no moth can destroy it.* **Wherever your treasure is, there the desires of your heart will also be**.
Luke 12:33-34 NLT

- Giving should be **generous and sacrificial**. Jesus taught about giving in the following passage from Luke:

    *Give, and you will receive. Your gift will return to you in full—**pressed down, shaken together** to make room for more, **running over**, and poured into your lap. The amount you give will determine the amount you get back. Luke 6:38 NLT*

    The imagery used will be familiar to anyone who's ever baked a cake, though in this case, Jesus was talking about selling grain in the marketplace. He said we should sell a measure of grain but press it down; shake it a bit to make sure it's completely full; then add more until it's running over and falling into your lap! Measuring like that would certainly bring your customers back, and that's the way Jesus expects us to give.

Do New Testament Believers need to tithe?

I realize I'm treading on dangerous ground, but it's really not possible to discuss giving to Kingdom needs without discussing the **TITHE**. While there are some who teach that the tithe is an Old Testament teaching and therefore not required of New Testament believers, my personal view is that seeing tithing as just an Old Testament command is short-sighted.

The tithe was established **before** the Old Testament Law of Moses. Though we're not sure when the concept originated, we do know that Abraham paid a tithe (tenth) to Melchizedek **long before** the Mosaic law, and **it's significant that the writer of Hebrews in the New Testament reminds us of the story**.

> *This Melchizedek was king of the city of Salem and also a priest of God Most High. When Abraham was returning home after winning a great battle against the kings,* ***Melchizedek met him and blessed him. Then Abraham took a tenth of all he had captured in battle and gave it to Melchizedek.*** *The name Melchizedek means "king of justice," and king of Salem means "king of peace."*
> *Hebrews 7:1-2 NLT*

Melchizedek is a one-of-a-kind character in the Old Testament who is generally accepted to be a "type" of Christ. If you aren't familiar with the term "typology", a "type" is an Old Testament representation of the character or action of Christ. Note that Melchizedek's name means King of Justice (sounds like Jesus, right?) and he was King of Salem (Jeru-Salem). Salem comes from the word *shalom,* meaning "peace". King of Justice, King of Peace. **The tithe was first recorded in Scripture as being given to the King of Justice and Peace.** That sounds like a pattern for worship to me.

The Bible doesn't say Melchizedek asked Abraham for anything. Abraham offered his tenth willingly as an honorarium to the King.

Under Moses, the people offered up **three tithes**, two of which were offered annually. The **first tithe** supported the priesthood – our equivalent of giving to the church. The **second annual tithe** was actually a set-aside to cover the cost of fulfilling a family's ministry obligations – like a mission-trip or ministry-vacation expense account. The **third tithe**, paid only every third year, was specifically given to support the poor – like a benevolence fund.

So, the Old Testament believer gave an average of 23% of their financial gain each year. What about New Testament believers? **IF** we tithe, we seem to argue whether it should be on our gross or net income! Jesus spoke a lot about how New Testament believers should live compared with those under the Old Testament Law when He shared the Sermon on the Mount *(Matthew 5-7)*.

In every case, what Jesus taught exceeded what was expected under the Law.

What does that say to us about our giving? Hint: might it mean that the tithe is a **starting point** for our giving to God?

The clearest passage in the Bible about tithing is in the Old Testament book of Malachi, but it contains additional insight beyond just giving a tithe to God:

> Bring **all the tithes** into the storehouse, that there may be food in My house, and **try Me** now in this," says the Lord of hosts, "If I will not open for you the windows of heaven and pour out for you such blessing that there will not be room enough to receive it. "And **I will rebuke the devourer for your sakes**, so that he will not destroy the fruit of your ground, nor shall the vine fail to bear fruit for you in the field," says the Lord of hosts….
> Malachi 3:10-11 NKJV

In the passage, God **challenges** us to put Him to the test – that's what the term "try Me" means. **What do you think God wants to prove** to us about tithing?

The second promise He makes regards the person He calls the "devourer". Whether the prophet is speaking about the person of Satan as the agent of destruction in the world or is personifying the 2nd Law of Thermodynamics (things tend to go from order to disorder), we all know that things wear out and break down over time. Is God implying through Malachi that He will somehow supernaturally make what we have left after we tithe last longer? Maybe.

God did use Moses to remind the Israelites of all the ways He had cared for them in the wilderness, including:

> ...I have led you **forty years** in the wilderness. **Your clothes have not worn out** on you, and **your sandals have not worn out** on your feet. *Deuteronomy 29:5 NLT*

Apparently, God "rebuked the devourer" for the Jews as they wandered in the wilderness. The whole idea reminds us that **the interaction between God's people and money involves the spiritual realm as well as the physical.** Our giving to God is an act of spiritual worship. God, in turn, acts on behalf of the giver to multiply or protect what remains, much like what Jesus did with the loaves and fish when He fed the five thousand.

One final thought about tithing after considering all that has been discussed:

> If you don't tithe, it's because **you believe you can do more** with a dollar than God can do with 90 cents.
> Think what you wish; **I'm betting on God**.

What could the Holy Spirit accomplish if every Believer followed Biblical principles and tithed? I think we can acknowledge that God could do amazing things even compared with the wonderful things God does now. One estimate is that as few as 10% of Christians actually tithe.[2] Are you willing to encourage others to trust God as faithful Stewards of all He provides? Perhaps a more appropriate question is whether you are willing **yourself** to be a more faithful steward of all God has entrusted to you?

---

[2] https://pushpay.com/blog/church-giving-statistics/

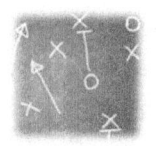

Strategy #4 – Invest spiritually in people by MENTORING them.

Time has become perhaps the most valuable commodity in our culture. Many workers will gladly accept time off from a job instead of additional pay. No one seems to have enough time to get the things accomplished that they desire. Doesn't it make sense, then, that **the currency of mentoring** is that most-precious commodity – **time**? God knows our time is extremely valuable, so if we spend it building into the lives of others, it shows the worth we place on mentoring. God thinks it's pretty important, too!

There is an easy equation to remember when calculating your mentoring efforts for the Kingdom of God:

Mentoring = Disciple-Making

While we may not think about our time invested at church and in the world as "disciple-making", that's exactly what mentoring to leave a spiritual legacy is all about. God has built truth into your life since you became a follower of Christ. Your life experiences deserve to be shared – both the good and successful ones as well as your regrettable mistakes. All of our personal and spiritual growth experiences can help the generations that follow us walk more uprightly with

God. Paul's protégé, Timothy, was encouraged to share his spiritual life experiences with others:

> *You have heard **me** teach things that have been confirmed by many reliable witnesses. Now teach these truths to **other trustworthy people** who will be able to pass them on to **others**.   2 Timothy 2:2 NLT*

Note the **4 generations of disciples** Paul mentions in that verse that were discussed earlier in this book: Paul, who had been teaching Timothy; Timothy, who should be teaching what he learned to "trustworthy people"; and the "others" who would receive the teaching from those "trustworthy" folks in whom Timothy had invested himself.

Called to Mentor

No one exemplified the mentor/discipler-lifestyle like Jesus, who spent more than three years, night and day, building into the lives of his closest followers. His words to His disciples after the resurrection make the command to mentor future generations inescapable:

> *So, wherever you go, **make disciples** of all nations: Baptize them in the name of the Father, and of the Son, and of the Holy Spirit. Teach them to do everything I have*

commanded you. Matthew 28:19-20 (God's Word Translation)

Most translations incorrectly emphasize the word "Go" in the passage we call "the Great Commission". There is **only one verb** in the command of Jesus – **to "make disciples"**. That command is followed by a series of infinitives – the "-ing" form of verbs. **Making disciples** then is accomplished by *Go<u>ing</u>, Baptiz<u>ing</u>, and Teach<u>ing</u>.*

The implication for each of us is this:

> **As we walk with God in our day-to-day living, we should be applying our faith and teaching in our relationships.**

Whether you feel like you've been actively fulfilling the Great Commission or not, Jesus challenges us to do something that should come very naturally.

How did you learn to tie your shoes? How did you learn to write your name? While both of those skills might have been learned long ago and you may not remember the actual learning experience, you know you didn't teach yourself. Someone invested time and energy in helping you learn early-in-life skills. Who is investing in early-in-new-life believers?

Not everyone who needs to be mentored is a new Christian, and not everyone who is a disciple-maker is a deep-thinking theologian. Most people in mentoring relationships are just like you and me – they just need to be matched up by skill level.

Once you've been convinced you **should be** a disciple-maker, it might be helpful to define a "disciple" in the simplest way possible:

| A Disciple is "**One who learns from another**" |

But is that enough to **fully understand** what Jesus meant when He used the term in the Bible?

| **Being a disciple of Jesus requires that we not only KNOW (intellectually), but that we WALK (practically) according to our faith.** |

Mentoring others isn't just about teaching them the truths found in the Bible. It's also about teaching them how to live. It's true that disciples must learn what you know, but they also need to see how you incorporate what you know into life. Learning about prayer isn't the same as praying with a mentor. Memorizing Scripture is wonderfully helpful but understanding how to apply it in life is much more important to the disciple of Christ.

Two fancy "church words" explain what becoming a disciple of Jesus means:

- Orthodoxy – means having right beliefs

- Orthopraxy – means living in the right way

Most people have at least heard the first word; the second is much less used. Both are vital and the apostle Paul wrote this to another of his protégés to make that point clear:

> And **you** yourself **must be an example** to them by doing good works of every kind. **Let everything you do** reflect the integrity and seriousness of your teaching. Teach the truth so that your teaching can't be criticized.
> Titus 2:7-8 NLT

Isn't that the biggest challenge we face as Mentors? WE are the example to those we disciple, though most of us feel woefully inadequate to the task. EVERYTHING we do must "reflect the integrity and seriousness" of what we teach them. On top of all that, we need to be certain that what we are passing along to them is absolutely true. I understand the great burden that might seem to place on each of us as Mentors, but the blessing of seeing your disciple grow into a mature follower of Christ outweighs any fears we might have.

**We must BE a disciple
before we can be a disciple-maker.**

Do you feel like you had a **qualified Mentor** in your life who helped you become a **faithful disciple**? If you did, it's likely you have no doubt about the value a mentor can provide. If you didn't, I'm confident you are aware of how much you missed. Every believer in Christ needs to have someone modeling spiritual integrity for them and pouring love and truth INTO their lives. Likewise, each of us needs another "someone" into whom we can share all we have discovered about walking with Christ.

Paul prayed often for those under his spiritual authority and his pattern should be a model for us. This passage from *Ephesians* shows the love he had for those who looked to him for direction:

> *I'm asking God to give you a gift from the wealth of his glory.* ***I pray that he would give you inner strength and power through his Spirit.*** *Then Christ will live in you through faith. I also pray that love may be the ground into which you sink your roots and on which you have your foundation. This way, with all of God's people you will be able to understand how wide, long, high, and deep his love is. You will know Christ's love,* ***which goes far beyond any knowledge.*** *I am praying this so that you may be completely filled with God. Ephesians 3:16-19. NOG*

Paul understood that disciples need **more than knowledge** about God. I believe our fear of being inadequate to the task is what stops many of us from undertaking the vital task of disciple-making. We understand our limitations, especially spiritually. Yet Paul's prayer for his disciples in Ephesus emphasized that the Holy Spirit was playing a role by empowering and infusing those who were seeking to grow under Paul's tutelage. Paul knew that though he was responsible to teach and model a life of faith, it is always God who brings the growth in the life of a disciple. Only the Spirit of God can make any disciple come to maturity.

> *I planted the seed in your hearts, and Apollos watered it, **but it was God who made it grow**. It's not important who does the planting, or who does the watering. What's important is that God makes the seed grow.*
> *1 Corinthians 3:6-7 NLT*

Paul wasn't just writing about the seed of salvation that had been planted in the Corinthians but was also referring to the growth they were enjoying under the guidance of others, like Apollos. Paul knew he wasn't the only person building into the lives of young believers.

> **NO ONE PERSON is responsible for bringing seekers to salvation and then leading them to maturity in the faith.**

We are ALL charged with the responsibility to make disciples of each new follower of Jesus. Paul was just reminding the Corinthians and us that we do what we can, but it is GOD who makes things real in our hearts and lives.

Our calling as Mentors isn't meant to be a burden but a joy. Our transparency with those we seek to disciple is a critical part of that process. We who would make disciples are fearful that our own flaws might derail the process, yet **allowing our own growth efforts to be apparent to those we seek to encourage helps them understand that process in their own lives**.

Paul put his own spiritual reputation on the line when he urged Timothy to observe him and how he lived:

> *But you, Timothy, certainly know **what I teach**, and **how I live**, and **what my purpose in life is**. You know my faith, my patience, my love, and my endurance. You know how much persecution and suffering I have endured…But you must remain faithful to the things you have been taught. **You know they are true, for you know you can trust those who taught you.**
> 2 Timothy 3:10-11,14 NLT*

It's common for us as believers to look at others in the Church and imagine they are much more mature and consistent in the faith than we are. Certainly, Paul was a wonderful mentor to Timothy. But Paul wasn't perfect. He made mistakes and misjudgments. He was powerful and fruitful, but not without his own flaws. Yet he challenged his most effective disciple, Timothy, to examine his life and faith carefully. Are you up to the challenge of building into the life of another fellow-disciple? Don't let fear or insecurity hold you back. What you know and how you live for Christ are worth sharing with others.

Choosing Our Disciples

Once you decide that **you're ready to be a disciple-maker**, how do you find someone to mentor?

- **Pray**. The Holy Spirit should make your choice clear if you listen. Jesus, who was always in tune with the Spirit of God, spent the night praying before naming those He would personally disciple. Even then He chose from among those who had already demonstrated a desire to follow Him:

    One day soon afterward Jesus went up on a mountain to pray, and ***he prayed to God all night***. *At daybreak he called together all of his disciples and* ***chose twelve*** *of them to be apostles. Luke 6:12-13 NLT*

- **Start small**. Choose one or two believers. Jesus only had 12. Think multiplication, not addition. You don't need a group of 30 to mentor to be considered a disciple-maker. If

Timothy followed Paul's admonition and chose three men to mentor and they, in turn, chose three more, the total would be a dozen men being mentored in their faith in the first cycle of discipleship.

*You have heard me teach things that have been confirmed by many reliable witnesses. Now **teach these truths to other trustworthy people who will be able to pass them on to others**. 2 Timothy 2:2 NLT*

- **Stay close.** Family is a good place to start. Children and grandchildren are prime targets for your mentoring efforts. If you aren't building faith into the lives of those closest to you, then you might not believe the importance of faith at all! Sometimes our lives don't provide direct descendants to mentor. If family members aren't a choice, consider those to whom you relate well. Who attends your church with whom you might connect? It's likely God has already placed your mentoring target in your life. Keep praying!

*And you must commit yourselves wholeheartedly to these commands that I am giving you today. **Repeat them again and again to your children**. Talk about them when you are **at home** and when you are **on the road**, when you are **going to bed** and when you are **getting up**. Tie them to your hands and wear* *them on your forehead as reminders.* **Write them on the doorposts of your house** *and on your gates. Deuteronomy 6:6-9 NLT*

- **Be prepared.** Your service is to God and your disciple. Nothing but your best should be offered. Because you are establishing yourself as a model to be followed, you need to be certain your walk with God is worthy of being emulated. Remember, you must BE a disciple before you can be a disciple-maker. Make sure you are closely following Christ.

    And ***you*** *yourself* ***must be an example*** *to them by doing good works of every kind.* <u>*Let everything you do*</u> *reflect the integrity and seriousness of your teaching. Teach the truth so that your teaching can't be criticized. Titus 2:7-8 NLT*

> **What do you need to improve to be prepared to Mentor someone?**

How do you approach someone and offer to mentor them? Often, the approach is less formal than that. The person who asks you questions after a class or small group is a prime candidate for mentoring. Family members who are new or young in the faith are ready for someone to help them grown. New believers "don't know what they don't know" yet, so they are not likely to seek out a mentor. But as a seasoned Follower of Jesus, you have the chance to invite them to meet with you and offer to begin their spiritual tutoring.

Still not sure what to do? Speak with your pastor and explain your willingness and seek his advice. Many times, there are individuals who have expressed a desire to grow in their walk with Christ and the pastor simply doesn't have the time to disciple everyone. You may offer to ease his burden by taking on the responsibility. **Trust me**, both God and the pastor will be pleased by your willingness.

Carrying out our Mission

You're ready and you've identified and recruited your mentoring candidate. Now what? Notice how many times Paul uses the word "taught" in this letter he wrote to the Ephesian church.

> *You have certainly **heard** his message and have **been taught** his ways. <u>The truth is in Jesus</u>. You were **taught** to change the way you were living...you were **taught** to have a new attitude. You were also **taught** to become a new person created to be like God, with a life that truly has God's approval and is holy. Ephesians 4:21-24 GW*

Remember "teaching" was a vital part of fulfilling the Great Commission. We are challenged in that passage to "*Teach them to do everything I have commanded you.*" You may not feel like you can teach others, but mentoring doesn't usually involve standing in front of a group and breaking down Scripture for them.

The Content

Discipling one-on-one or one-on-two is much different than trying to lead a larger group. The teaching is more conversational. It's often driven by the questions coming from the disciple. You only need to know **what you already know** to be a good mentor. John wrote this to his own disciples later in his life:

> *The Word of life existed from the beginning.* ***We have heard it. We have seen it. We observed and touched it.*** *This life was revealed to us. We have seen it, and* ***we testify about it.*** *We are reporting to you about this eternal life that was in the presence of the Father and was revealed to us. This is the life we have seen and heard. We are reporting about it* ***to you also so that you, too, can have a relationship with us.*** *Our relationship is with the Father and with his Son Jesus Christ. 1 John 1: 1-3. GW*

What do we teach those whom we mentor? What we have heard and seen. Why do we do it? So that those we disciple can enjoy a fuller relationship with us and with the Father, the Son, and the Holy Spirit.

Share what you have been studying in your own quiet time each day. Discuss your thoughts about the latest sermon at church or Bible teaching in the men's or women's groups at church. Challenge the person you're mentoring to read the best Christian-living book you've read and discuss their impressions. Ask them what they'd like to know and help them find the answers. WHAT you teach is less important than THAT you teach. Over time, the content will cover much of what they need to learn. Believe me when I say that your efforts in trying to teach them about Scripture will result in you becoming much stronger and confident in your own faith. What a great side-effect, right? God's plan for disciple-making causes BOTH parties to grow stronger in their faith and in their walk with Jesus.

The Game Plan

When all the pieces of your mentoring plan begin to come together, when and where do you execute your game plan? Depending on what format you've chosen, whether to work with people individually or try to meet with 2-3 disciples as a group, find a location that fits your needs.

A public place is always best, even though a Mentor should always only work with disciples of the same sex. Offering to meet in your home or one belonging to a participant may work after you've established relationships, but isn't the best idea initially. Before you know one another well, the intimacy of a home location might be too intimidating for some disciples to accept.

Head to McDonalds or Starbucks or meet in a public area at your church. As long as you can carry on a spiritual conversation and spend a few minutes in prayer without being disturbed or bothering those around you, the location should work for everyone.

Limit the meeting time before you begin. Your disciple will want to understand the time commitment before accepting an invitation to be discipled. YOU need to establish parameters for your effort as well since your time is also valuable. I'd suggest 45 minutes to an hour to start. More than that initially might seem too long. You may find that by mutual agreement you'd like to go longer, though I would suggest a limit of 90 minutes for any particular session.

Don't try to do so much that it can't be processed. The goal isn't to offload as much information as possible in the shortest amount of time.

> **Ultimately, your purpose in mentoring is for your disciple to see you living out your faith.**

Allow enough time for those you mentor to "catch" what you are offering. Mentoring isn't intended to be a speedy process. Jesus spent three and a half years, night and day with His disciples. Don't expect to accomplish your disciple-making goals more quickly than the Master.

Begin your first gathering by sharing your own testimony. Ask each person to do the same as a means of introduction. Then proceed to work through a Bible text or book. Seek help from your pastor or discipleship director for help with ideas or curriculum materials. Using a curriculum to provide guidance and flow is a great idea. Your church should have such materials available.

Establish your meeting schedule BEFORE you begin. Once weekly is a great way to start, but set a beginning date and ending date before you begin so your disciples know the length of their commitment to you. Sometimes, your choice of those to mentor might not work out as you had hoped. A pre-determined length for the initial experience allows everyone to re-set their Game Plan if the encounters don't seem fruitful.

Remember: God is the One who is bringing about any growth in the life of the disciple. You are only the tool He is using.

Our faithfulness in seeking to share our life of faith with those who come behind us is what honors God.

Our discussion has centered around being the "Paul" in some "Timothy's" life by providing mentoring. **But who is mentoring you?** Paul had those who taught him; Timothy had Paul; Timothy's protégés were learning from him while still teaching others. It is certainly important for us to be building into the lives of others in fulfillment of the Great Commission. But WE continually need to be challenged in our own faith experience.

To find your own mentor, take all these ideas to help you find someone to disciple and then apply them in reverse, so you are able to have a mentor in your life. Your growth should never stop just because you have grown and matured yourself. Giving spiritually while never receiving isn't healthy. **Be a mentor, but always continue being a disciple!**

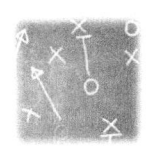

Strategy #5 – Determine to leave a lasting LEGACY of Faith.

If you've made it to the 4th Quarter of your life, you have, no doubt, begun to think about your legacy. You may not be that old yet, but this is the perfect time to begin to create a strategy to allow you to leave behind something spiritually significant when you depart for heaven. If you've begun to implement the first four strategies, you're already well on your way to creating a lasting spiritual legacy

One writer says, "I know that within three generations after my death, I will be just a faceless name on a sheet of paper. I'm OK with that. But I want to pass on the **Living Legacy of Christ** I received so it will continue to provide a positive impact on those who come behind me **for many generations**."

Those words epitomize the heartbeat of **Strategy #5**. To be able to utilize all the aspects of our Christian experience – our Faith, Ministry, Stewardship, and Mentoring – to finally see things come together in the spiritual Legacy we leave is what our lives are supposed to be about. We will likely be forgotten by generations to come. But the imprint we leave on those succeeding generations could be immeasurable if we are successful in leaving a spiritual legacy.

Stay focused on this truth: A Legacy is NOT a résumé or a list of personal or spiritual accomplishments.

A Legacy Is the Imprint You Leave On the Future.

The concept of Legacy isn't anything new to people of Faith. A great story that illustrates that truth appears in the early part of Genesis concerning Abraham:

> Then **Abraham planted a tamarisk tree** at Beersheba, and there **he worshiped the Lord, the Eternal God.** Genesis 21:33 NLT

We might typically focus on the latter part of the verse and remark about Abraham's worship of God. And then note, "Oh yeah, Abraham planted a tree, too." That's the kind of statement in the Bible that we usually just pass right over.

But the tamarisk tree is unique. It's a desert plant intended to help those who live near it to find **cooling rest** under its branches. The salty nature of its evergreen needles is different from the other trees found in the desert areas south of Jerusalem. Those needles attract moisture that can then be released during the day to provide cooling to those near it.

But the tree is also special because it grows VERY slowly – only about an inch each year. One inch. It can take a tamarisk tree **400-500 years to reach its full size!**

It's obvious Abraham didn't plant the tree for Isaac, or his grandchildren, or even his great-grandchildren, but for the generations that would follow them.

"Then Abraham planted a tamarisk tree at Beersheba, and there he worshiped the LORD, the Eternal God." Genesis 21:33

It's conceivable that the Israelites who fled Egypt many generations later found rest under that very tree. Abraham understood acting on behalf of future generations. Do we fully understand the impact we can have?

Abraham's simple act of planting a tree in the desert was a demonstration of his Faith and belief in doing things NOW with an eye towards the future.

While you may not currently be planting trees as acts of faith, **what is YOUR idea of what it means to "plant a Tamarisk tree" today?**

Spiritual Legacy

The magnitude of your spiritual legacy can't be determined in the present, but **it is being DECIDED by what you DO in the present.** Some may not set out to leave a lasting spiritual impact, they just never stop laboring effectively for Christ and the result is that they DO leave a tremendous spiritual inheritance. Most of us continue to serve Christ in some manner, but we should ask ourselves **if we are doing the things that will have the greatest impact on generations to come.**

God's timing is impeccable. As I write this chapter, I am less than 24 hours from my mother's funeral. Yesterday her grandchildren stood and reminisced about her impact on their lives – on the spiritual legacy she left in them. They were able to share about her faith and her challenge to them to live in ways that honored God. Everyone reading this has either lost or will lose their parents. The timing of that life-changing event is one of the issues faced by 4th Quarter adults, and it should remind us of the importance of the spiritual legacy that WE hope to leave.

Our efforts to leave a godly legacy aren't intended to focus on praise from our fellow church-goers in the here-and-now. Instead, we must allow ourselves to be driven by a **mindset focused on eternity**. Paul's efforts in the lives of those he sought to impact became obvious to him and everyone else:

> *The only letter of recommendation we need is you yourselves.* ***Your lives are a letter written in our hearts;*** *everyone can read it and recognize our good work among you. Clearly,* ***you are a letter from Christ showing the result of our ministry among you.*** *This "letter" is written not with pen and ink, but with the Spirit of the living God. It is carved not on tablets of stone, but* ***on human hearts****.*
> 2 Corinthians 3:2-3 NLT

Isn't that what we each want? To know that God has used us in dynamic ways to touch the lives of others? If so, begin now to pray for God's answer to the following question:

What can I do NOW that will make the most difference in the next generation, and the next after that?
THAT is what we must plan for.

Because what we do **today** determines our Spiritual Legacy, we should be **walking faithfully** with Christ in each of the areas we've discussed:

- **FAITH** – do people see God when they watch how we live? Do we seem to fully grasp and embrace everything the Gospel of Grace brings into our lives? Does everyone around us KNOW what we believe and understand what it means for THEM to trust Christ?

- **MINISTRY** – are we serving and loving everyone selflessly? Have we discovered and developed the gift for ministry provided by the Holy Spirit? Are we effectively using our gift?

- **STEWARDSHIP** – are we gathering and sharing the resources God entrusts to us? Are we giving faithfully to Kingdom projects? Are we living carefully and seeking God's guidance for the surplus wealth He provides?

- **MENTORING** – are we making faithful disciples? Are we making ANY disciples? Have we spent enough time seeking out and building into the lives of the people that God has placed in our paths? If I have children and grandchildren, am I helping them follow after Christ?

No one but Jesus has done a perfect job of handling all those aspects to leave a perfect Legacy, but we're still here so there's <u>still time to make a difference</u>!

If I want to make sure I've left a spiritual Legacy, what can I do?

- <u>Serve</u>. Our church's **4th Quarter Team** has a goal to have 100% of our participants engaged in ministry. I encourage you to challenge those in your church to do the same. Teach; encourage; pray; take a mission trip. **Everyone can do something, but no one can do everything!** We are a part of the Body of Christ, so whatever we do may not be completed in our lifetimes, but God has that under control.

For we are both God's workers. And you are God's field. You are God's building. Because of God's grace to me, I have laid the foundation like an expert builder. **Now others are building on it***. But whoever is building on this foundation must be very careful.   1 Corinthians 3:9-10 NLT*

- **Share**. Only those who hear the Gospel can respond. Write a letter to someone who needs to clearly understand your trust in Jesus and who **needs to hear how they, too, can believe**. If you're a little more tech-savvy, consider **uploading your testimony to YouTube** for the generations that will follow you. Make sure that your children and grandchildren have heard the Gospel. If you haven't shared, who else do you expect will?

I remember your genuine faith, for you share the faith that first filled your grandmother Lois and your mother, Eunice. And I know that **same faith** *continues strong in you.   2 Timothy 1:5 NLT*

- **Invest**. Live carefully so you can give faithfully. Sponsor a child through a trusted ministry; plan your inheritance in a way that **you control your Legacy**. If you decide to leave all the accumulated wealth God has provided to your children and grandchildren, that's your choice. But consider that **YOU are the one God entrusted with those funds** and those who follow you might not have the same values and vision as you. What joy there is in giving to Kingdom projects!

"Don't store up treasures here on earth, where moths eat them and rust destroys them, and where thieves break in and steal. ***Store your treasures in heaven****, where moths and rust cannot destroy, and thieves do not break in and steal.* ***Wherever your treasure is, there the desires of your heart will also be.***
Matthew 6:19-21 NLT

Financial Legacy

Having just "crossed the line" by bringing up your money, let me go further and speak to an issue that is rarely discussed, especially among 4th Quarter adults. This is the question you might pose to me: **"What responsibility do I have as a Christian to leave behind an inheritance for my children or a financial legacy for the Kingdom of God?"** For context, one source says that only 56% of retirees plan to leave any inheritance for their children. Are the rest all wrong or are they just planning to spend everything they have on themselves?

Let's address the first part of the question first. The Bible says this about inheritance for children and grandchildren:

> ***Good people leave an inheritance to their grandchildren****, but the sinner's wealth passes to the godly.   Proverbs 13:22 NLT*

Does that mean whatever financial wealth I have left when I die needs to pass on to my grandchildren? What about my children? What if I don't have either, then what?

As you can tell from my approach in other areas, I believe the Bible is clear and truthful in presenting God's plan for every area of our lives. This particular passage from Proverbs, though, leaves us with relatively little instruction other than the encouragement that the godly will leave an inheritance, while the ungodly will in some way forfeit theirs. Proverbs is **meant to convey wisdom** to the reader and not necessarily detailed financial advice.

My take-away from Proverbs 13?

> **God intends to financially bless the Godly.**

I can hear you saying, "Wait a minute, that sounds too much like those who teach a 'prosperity Gospel'." Perish the thought! Then who are these godly people that God is blessing financially? **Those who follow after God and obey His principles and live according to His precepts.** Remember that Proverbs conveys God's perspective on life to us. Some of us might not feel "financially blessed" by God. Why is that? Could it be because we HAVEN'T faithfully obeyed God's principles and lived according to His precepts?

Have you **ever** co-signed for anyone to get a loan? Have you **ever** passed up the opportunity to take on more work to make a bit extra? Have you **always** laid aside a portion of what you earned for your future needs? Have you **ever** carried a balance on a credit card account or borrowed money for any purpose other than to buy a home? Have you **ever** lived paycheck-to-paycheck? If you have failed in any of these areas, you HAVE NOT always "followed after God and obeyed His principles and lived according to His precepts", according to the book of *Proverbs*.

Should our lives be considered failures if we've not been totally obedient in the area of finances? No more than our failures in other areas negate our salvation. Each and every failure in our lives is covered by the blood of Christ, including those financial mis-deeds that have caused us to make one or more of the mistakes listed above.

What is the key to avoiding personal financial mistakes? Taking these words Paul wrote to Timothy to heart:

> Yet **true godliness with contentment is itself great wealth.** After all, we brought nothing with us when we came into the world, and we can't take anything with us when we leave it. So if we have enough food and clothing, **let us be content.** But **people who long to be rich fall into temptation** and are trapped by many foolish and harmful desires that plunge them into ruin and destruction. For **the love of money is the root of all kinds of evil.** And some people, craving money, have wandered from the true faith and pierced themselves with many sorrows. 1 Timothy 6:6-10 NLT

Lack of contentment is what drives us to borrow funds or use a credit card to purchase things we can't afford. Lack of contentment is what drives others to ask us to co-sign for them so they can do the same thing with poor credit. If banks won't lend money to your relatives because they are poor credit risks, why do you think you know better?

When we spend all we have and don't save for the future, it's because we are unwilling to wait for God to provide what we THINK we need.

God is either able to provide for your needs or He isn't. When you use credit to purchase something you want because God hasn't provided the funds yet, you are either denying God's provision or admitting your own lack of contentment.

As incomes increase and overall wealth is generally increasing, **giving to our churches is actually going down.** Religious giving is down 50% since 1990. The average Christian gives only 2.5% of his income to the church but during the Great Depression the average church-goer contributed over 3%! And **if you believe you'd be able to give more if you only made more**, among families making more than $75,000 per year only 1% give at least a tithe.[3] One in a hundred. It's sad to learn that people who make less than $20,000 are **8x as likely to tithe** as those who make more than $75,000, so income has nothing to do with our giving patterns – **faith does**. God doesn't care how much money you make. He cares about how much you trust and believe in His provision.

The ability to leave a financial legacy requires us to master the chapter on Stewardship first. Without following Biblical advice on finances, we will have nothing to share as a legacy. Overcoming our lack of contentment is equally vital to leaving a financial legacy to serve the Kingdom for years to come.

---

[3] https://pushpay.com/blog/church-giving-statistics/

> If you are a 4th Quarter adult,
> **it is NOT TOO LATE to prepare
> to leave a financial legacy**.

By following these steps, you'll find new freedom to contribute significantly to advance God's Kingdom rather than being bound up by the chains of debt. Here's what you need to do:

1. **Get out of debt.** Programs like Financial Peace University[4] will help you take the necessary steps. You can't be fully available to God is you are stuck in debt. I know from personal experience that we sometimes have to say "No" to the leading of God because we are in bondage to a lender.

   *Just as the rich rule the poor, so **the borrower is servant to the lender**. Proverbs 22:7 NLT*

2. **If you don't currently tithe, give to God increasingly until you are giving at least 10%.** If you have questions about tithing, go back and read the chapter on Stewardship. Tithing demonstrates your trust and dependence on God for all you have. By giving Him your first-fruits, **you accept His challenge** to make the 90% you keep go further than if you had kept all your resources.

---

[4] https://www.daveramsey.com/store/product/financial-peace-university-class

> ***Bring all the tithes*** *into the storehouse…If you do," says the Lord of Heaven's Armies, "I will open the windows of heaven for you. I will pour out a blessing so great you won't have enough room to take it in!* ***Try it! Put me to the test!*** *Malachi 3:10 NLT*

If you don't tithe now and don't trust God enough to start immediately, begin to give an ever-increasing amount and see how God responds. If you calculate you're currently only giving 2% of your income, commit to giving 4%. If you're giving 7% commit to 9%. You get the idea. **God wants us to grow in our faith**, and when we give faithfully to His causes and ministries, we discover that our gifts are making a difference for eternity and we didn't miss the money. In fact, seeing the result of our giving makes us more committed to giving in even greater ways.

3. **Begin to dream about ways to invest to leave a Financial Legacy for the Kingdom of God**. You may have heard the saying, "Man plans, and God laughs." But when we dream about ways to build and serve the Kingdom, God is right there with us. Our dreams won't even do justice to what God can do through what may seem to us an insignificant gift.

> *Now **all glory to God, who is able**, through his mighty power at work within us, **to accomplish infinitely more than we might ask or think**.* Ephesians 3:20 NLT

Ask yourself, "What am I willing to believe God can do through my lifetime of careful living and saving?"

> **This is the time in life when CAREFUL STEWARDSHIP allows you to plant seeds that will last FOREVER.**

I must admit to you that financially-careful living has not been a lifetime pursuit for me. Like many who grew up in post-World War 2 America, it seemed like the world was mine for the taking. As a child, we enjoyed our lives and though my family lived paycheck-to-paycheck, we never went without anything we needed. My family never had extra funds, so I never learned about budgeting and saving. Perhaps you had a similar experience?

As an adult, I have always been generous in my giving, especially to the church. God has shown Himself faithful as I have tithed since I understood what it meant. But my financial carelessness in other ways and family demands in my earlier adult years caused me to ignore preparing for a future legacy. In recent years, I've gained an eternal perspective on my finances and I've been able to be a better steward of what God has provided.

> **The transition wasn't easy, but God has shown me what I can "do without" for the sake of His Kingdom needs.**

Providing for Kingdom projects doesn't require that you accumulate millions of dollars in life and then leave it all to the church at your death. Giving, even in small ways, can make an eternal difference.

Scripture records a fantastic story about a woman named Tabitha and her impact on those to whom she gave:

> There was a believer in Joppa named **Tabitha** (which in Greek is Dorcas). **She was always doing kind things for others and helping the poor.** About this time she became ill and died. Her body was washed for burial and laid in an upstairs room. But the believers had heard that Peter was nearby at Lydda, so they sent two men to beg him, "Please come as soon as possible!" So Peter returned with them; and as soon as he arrived, they took him to the upstairs room. **The room was filled with widows who were weeping and showing him the coats and other clothes Dorcas had made for them.** Acts 9:36-39 NLT

The text continues to describe how Peter was so greatly moved by the kindness Tabitha had shown to others that he prayed, and she was raised from the dead! My focus, however, is that she engaged in acts of kind giving, even making clothes and coats for those who needed them. She wasn't rich but she invested what she had with an eternal perspective.

What if you are blessed with sufficient finances to do more than just make or buy clothes for the poor? What are some **simple ways to help make an eternal difference** for Christ?

- Give to your church's mission offering or help **support a missionary family directly**.

- **Sponsor a child** through World Vision[5] or Compassion International[6], both Christian agencies working in 3rd World countries.

- Help offer a child a **Christian education** and other support by sponsoring a **Samuel's Fund child through STCH Ministries**[7].

- Pack a **shoebox** to take the Gospel to a child somewhere in the world via **Operation Christmas Child**[8]. Better still, pack a dozen if you can.

---

[5] https://www.worldvision.org/sponsor-a-child

[6] https://www.compassion.com/sponsor_a_child/

[7] https://www.stchm.org/international/samuels-fund-sponsorships/

[8] https://www.samaritanspurse.org/what-we-do/operation-christmas-child/

- Donate to your local **Christian food bank**. Why not sign up to help them, allowing you to more carefully oversee your investment?

I could obviously go on and on. You can easily find ways to invest in your local church, your local area, or give to needs outside your reach by investing in worldwide ministries that honor Christ. Do your homework and make certain your gift is getting to your project with very little fundraising cost. Choose quality, transparent ministries in which to invest.

> **Don't lose sight of the fact that while your gifts might seem like simple "giving" to everyone else, you are following your 4TH QUARTER STRATEGY by "investing" with eternal goals in mind.**

Income Tax Issues Related to Giving

While it might not seem "spiritual" to discuss the Internal Revenue Service in the same breath as spiritual legacies, there are practical considerations related to our topic that should be recognized. My personal accountant, a former pastor, has as his office motto "Render unto Caesar what is Caesar's and not a penny more!" Both Biblical and practical.

Having already discussed the decline in overall giving in the last 30 years and the fact that many high-earning individuals don't give much of their wealth to charities anyway, some recent changes in the IRS tax code have made giving even less attractive for those of us with "normal" incomes.

> **Don't forget that WE GIVE TO GOD, not because we get a tax deduction, but because we desire to HONOR HIM.**

I believe we have an obligation to tithe whether we can deduct it or not. But there ARE financial strategies that enable Christian taxpayers to give and still be able to take full advantage of our tax laws. While I do advise you to consult your accountant regarding any tax-saving financial decisions you make, there are two options I'd like to make you aware of that will help you plan for your financial legacy.

Bunching

The current IRS tax code starting in 2018 raised the standard deduction to higher levels while eliminating certain personal exemptions. The ultimate result will be that the vast majority of people will not itemize on their federal tax return. Charitable giving is one of the key deductions if you've itemized in the past. If getting credit for your giving disappears, the fear is that many people will give less, if they continue to give at all.

"Bunching" allows you to pack one tax year with deductible expenses providing you with total deductions that are high enough to exceed your standard deduction. You are able to itemize for things like your home mortgage, medical expenses, taxes, and charitable giving, among other things.

Bunching is accomplished by lumping many of the deductible expenses into the same tax year by:

- Paying your **property taxes** for next year **early**. This may result in paying two years of taxes in the same year, but that's what "bunching" is all about.

- Giving your **tithe** at the end of this year **for the next year.** It's likely your church won't be upset to get the funds in advance, but perhaps let the pastor know so they don't view the extra money as a "windfall".

- Making **large purchases** (like a car) in the same year as other deductible expenses so you can deduct the tax paid on the item.

- Donate to a **Donor-Advised Fund** which will be discussed in more detail in the next section.

Mention **bunching** to your tax advisor and he will provide you with more ideas and help you work through the process to be able to maximize your deductions to help reduce your tax burden. Is it right to use whatever means are available to us to be certain we avoid paying more taxes than necessary? It was Jesus who told us to *"render to Caesar that which is Caesar's"*, but Jesus also said,

> Look, I am sending you out as sheep among wolves. So **be as shrewd as snakes and harmless as doves**. Matthew 10:16 NLT

As Christians, we must be examples to others in our adherence to the laws of the land. Likewise, as good stewards, we must be committed to being wise and even shrewd, if necessary. Make every dollar count for the Kingdom of God.

Legacy-Giving Options

If you follow my advice and speak with your tax preparer about a **Donor-Advised Fund (DAF)**, don't be surprised if the initial response is, "What?" My financial advisor had never heard of a DAF until I presented it as an option for my Legacy Giving. Though they have been a giving option for many years, DAFs simply aren't that well-known yet.

I have invested in a DAF[9] and I see it as a wonderful strategy to use whatever wealth I have and will accumulate for the spread of the Gospel. There are

---

[9] https://www.tropericecharitable.org/

numerous well-branded DAFs available from which to choose, so do sufficient research or get great advice before choosing your fund. Generally, establishing a DAF is a little like starting your own Charitable Trust Fund, though actually setting up a Trust is quite complicated and has long-term responsibilities that are not required when investing in a DAF.

Typical steps in the process of establishing your DAF are:

1. **Choose a company.** Each Fund may charge a small fee for their services, but the amount is usually negligible. Mine charges 0.5% annually on balances below $500,000 (that catches me, for sure) and if you have more money to contribute than that, the annual fee goes down.

2. **Make an initial contribution.** The money you give is a gift, no different than if you give it to the Red Cross or your church. Once given, the money is not yours any longer. That irreversible aspect to the gift is what qualifies you to deduct the FULL AMOUNT of the gift in the year in which it is GIVEN. Different funds may require different initial gift amounts to establish the DAF. All funds have their information available online.

3. **Recommend a Grant gift.** The funds you donated are now available for you, the Donor, to Advise for giving. Our recommendations are made online and may be designated to be given to any USA charity. Our DAF site allows us to look

up potential charities before giving a gift to them. Grant recommendations require minimum gift amounts, but normally fall well within the needs budgets of most givers.

My personal experience is that using the DAF has permitted me to "bunch" my gifts and be able to itemize on my taxes when it would otherwise not be possible. We gave our tithe for THIS year to the DAF at the end of last year, and this year, our church receives a grant check monthly. I could have asked for the gift to be granted more or less often, but monthly works for me. We've also been able to give other gifts, allowing us to support a child and an orphanage project in the Dominican Republic by working through a US-based charity.

As long as your grant request is sufficiently large (our minimum grant is $100), the grant is paid almost immediately upon presenting an online request. Essentially, a DAF is a savings account for your giving, providing you with full, immediate tax-deductibility in the year you give your gift. You won't get double credit for your gift when it is paid through the DAF because your gift to the DAF has already resulted in a tax deduction.

Three other great benefits of a DAF:
- Because gifts are given through the DAF, they **can be given anonymously** while the giver still receives a tax deduction. My DAF gives

me the option to send any gift without including my personal information. This also allows you to give a single gift **without being bombarded** by future gift requests from that particular charity or to give all gifts to your church or others anonymously to meet the Biblical admonition to *"not let your left hand know what your right hand is doing."* (Matthew 6:3)

- Funds given to your DAF can be **invested within the fund** to continue to grow the amount of your gift, if that is your desire.

- It's possible to establish **joint- or successor-Donor-Advisors**[10] who can take over your fund even after your death to continue your giving for years after you have been promoted to heaven. This is a fantastic way to involve your children or other close friends or relatives in your spiritual giving plan.

Another option if you've acquired enough assets that you know you'd like to leave to a specific charity, typically $100,000+, is to establish a **Charitable Remainder Trust (CRT)**.[11] This is a unique giving instrument that allows you to bypass creating your own family trust (normally only done when donating millions of dollars), yet create a trust fund that will

---

[10] https://www.tropricecharitable.org/benefits.html

[11] https://www.nolo.com/legal-encyclopedia/charitable-trust-tax-deduction-break-29702.html

pass on any remaining balance to your designated donor at your death or that of a surviving spouse.

The CRT comes in two different forms, one which pays a fixed dollar amount annually (CRAT) and one which pays a fixed percentage of the fund balance each year (CRUT). Most people opt for the CRUT since funds are invested and can actually grow your gift once it's been designated. The IRS actually requires a CRT to pay out **at least 5%** annually (very competitive with insurance-based annuities), but that rate can be negotiated to even higher levels based on different factors, including your life expectancy when the donation occurs. Besides the annual income received from the CRT, you'll **also receive a Charitable Giving deduction** for the year in which the gift to the trust is actually committed. The deduction won't be for the full value of the gift since the charity will only receive what is left in the fund upon your death, hence the term Charitable *Remainder* Trust.

How can you set up a CRT for your Legacy Giving Program?

- **Reach out to the charity** of your choice and work with them to identify their Trustee of choice. There is no upfront cost to establish the CRT.
- **Work with the trust firm to determine the details** of your gift, including the amount, the amount of return promised, the length of the

commitment (for a single life or joint life, if married), and the allowable tax deduction for the gift.

- **Enjoy some financial return on your gift** for the rest of your life, knowing the balance will pass on to the charity you believe is doing precious work in advancing the Kingdom of God.

In sharing information about any financial topic, please understand that I have no financial interest, nor do I receive any compensation for anything I've passed along to you. I simply wish to share with you the ideas that have worked for me. Each of us is responsible to make the right choices regarding our future and our finances. No one has all the answers, but your Bible, your family, your accountant, and hopefully this book can provide help in your quest.

Last thoughts about Finances and Family

My children are amazing. I guess every father says that, but my children are, in order of spiritual importance:

- Followers of Jesus
- Loving and kind people and gentle parents
- High-character adults (I guess that SHOULD go without saying since they are Believers)
- Giving and generous

- Well-educated, bright, and successful in their fields

While I understand the impact parenting has had on them, God is the One who gets the credit for their success in every area. I've said all that to bring our discussion to this point:

> **What is my financial responsibility to my adult children going forward?**

As wonderful as they are, I believe my answer according to Scripture is…none. Like most of us, I was able to provide for my children when they were growing up; I was blessed that they could attend Christian schools; and funds were available to help them through University. When the time comes for me to depart this life to enjoy my eternal reward, I DO anticipate being able to leave some "fun money" for my kids. I suppose they will plan to do the same for their children. But do I owe them more than that? Should they receive **everything** that God has blessed me with as a faithful steward?

> *The **servant** to whom he had entrusted the five bags of silver came forward with five more and said, 'Master, you gave me five bags of silver to invest, and I have earned five more.' "The master was full of praise. **'Well done, my good and faithful servant. You have been faithful in handling this small amount, so***

113

now I will give you many more responsibilities. Matthew 25:20-21 NLT

This passage of Scripture is only part of a parable that is familiar to most Christians. This particular servant was the most productive of the three in the story, doubling the money he was given by the Master. The second servant in the story was given less, but he also doubled what he had. The third servant failed to provide any gain for the Master from the funds he had been provided.

> **"Good and Faithful" are based on HOW the steward HANDLED money, not on how much he made.**

How does the parable relate to whether we should leave any accumulated wealth to our heirs? It is OUR job to be good stewards of all that God provides to US. It is required that our children learn to be good stewards of all God gives THEM. If God entrusted YOU with the resources you have, YOU should be the one to decide how best to use them. Your children will hopefully be blessed as well and be used by God as stewards of His resources IF they have learned the lessons from YOUR life of faithful stewardship.

If you are using the resources God has provided to you for His Kingdom projects to bail out your adult children because they are failing to follow the principles and precepts of God, I fear you may soon experience reduced flow from the fountain of God's material blessing into your own life. Jesus said, *"Because you have been a **faithful steward**, I'll give you more responsibilities."* Apparently, our usefulness as a steward is contingent on our faithfulness to use what God gives for HIS purposes. Our children must meet the same standard to receive the same blessing from God.

It will be my joy to ask my children to serve as successor-Advisors for my Donor-Advised Fund. We will be able to spend time in prayer together asking God to show us how to use what He has provided. My children will learn my values in giving and if I haven't been able to gift all my God-given resources before I depart this life, then my kids will receive the blessing of being able to provide gifts from my DAF to those whom God selects. I know they have generous hearts, and I know they will find as much joy in leaving a Financial Legacy as I do.

Strategy #6 – Strive to work as HARD as you can for as LONG as you can.

Sage advice can be found throughout the pages of Scripture, like this passage from the book of Hezekiah that you've heard since you were young:

> *Early to bed and early to rise,*
> *Makes a man healthy, wealthy and wise.*

OK, there is no book of Hezekiah and the quote is from Ben Franklin's *Poor Richard's Almanac*. I was just making sure you're still paying attention after all that financial information in the last chapter because what comes next is what makes everything work.

In some ways, **Strategy #6** could be seen as **the key to 4th Quarter living**. Each of the first five strategies should be a part of **every Christian's life plan**:

- Understanding the depth of our **faith**;
- Committing to serve diligently in the **ministry** area for which we are gifted;
- Carefully spending and saving as good **stewards**;
- Investing the time and energy necessary to **mentor** those who follow us in the faith;

- Planning for the spiritual and financial **legacies** we will leave for the next generations of Believers.

Each of these strategies will make our lives more fruitful for the kingdom.

> **Yet how might your fruitfulness be affected by the DEPTH and LENGTH of your commitment to Jesus?**

If you serve the Kingdom for some period of time and then stop because you decide you've done enough, can you recognize how that might affect the harvest produced by your life? If you are young and living a busy life filled with work and family and fun and you delay your leap into Christian servanthood, can you see how that will lessen your lifetime productivity for the Kingdom? Taking ourselves "out of the game" for any period of time will impact the harvest our lives produce.

Long-Term Commitment

God is at work in the life of every Believer long before we come to faith. God prepares our hearts, brings conviction to our lives, provides someone to share the Gospel with us, uses the circumstances of our lives to plow the hard ground of receptivity, and then, when all things are ready, He infuses our lives with Faith and our Spirits are reborn.

> ***God saved you*** *by his grace when you believed. And* ***you can't take credit for this****; it is a gift from God.* ***Salvation is not a reward*** *for the good things we have done, so none of us can boast about it. For we are God's masterpiece. He has created us anew in Christ Jesus,* ***so we can do the good things he planned for us long ago.***
> Ephesians 2:8-10 NLT

Just like the Mentoring we do in the lives of others, God prepares us for Faith by doing the same in our lives through the power of the Holy Spirit. HE is doing it. While you might think you reasoned your way to faith and made the decision completely on your own, you are mistaken.

The power of God brings sinful people to the fountain of grace to receive the free gift of salvation.

In the same way, God has prepared us for lives of service *"so we can do the good things he planned for us long ago."* How do we accomplish them?

Jesus spoke to His disciples on the night Judas betrayed Him about what would happen to them after

He was crucified. How would they become more productive and remain so?

> "Yes, I am the vine; you are the branches. **Those who remain in me, and I in them, will produce much fruit.** For apart from me you can do nothing." John 15:5 NLT

Some might read the passage and confuse the meaning of the word "remain". Another favored translation of the same word in the passage is "abide". Both seem to conjure the idea of "being" or "residing" in Jesus. We are all, of course, "in Christ" **positionally** once we come to faith. But the verse in context isn't speaking about our spiritual position as Christians, it's speaking about **our commitment** as Christians.

According to *Thayer's Greek Lexicon*, the verb in the passage translated *"remain"* as it references the passing of time for a Believer means: *"to last, **to endure**: of persons, **to live**"*.

Jesus was speaking about whether His disciples would continue to live out their faith and complete the work they had begun with Him.

What Jesus shared was essentially His 4th Quarter speech to the disciples!

Put yourself in the room and listen to what Jesus shared that night as documented by John:

- **He promised them a place** WITH Him after they finished the work to which they were called *(John 14)*.
- **He promised them fruitfulness** IF they continued to be committed to His cause *(John 15)*.
- **He warned them** about what would lie ahead for them, acknowledging that the task wouldn't be easy, but reminding them that **they would be victorious because of the Power in them** *(John 16)*.

What do the words, *"Those who **remain** in me, and I in them, will produce much fruit"* mean for you? They constitute a challenge:

> **To LIVE for Christ,**
> **Not just today, but EVERY day; Not just when you feel like it, but even when you don't; Not just when the game looks winnable, but especially when it doesn't.**

Belonging TO Christ is enough to get you to heaven. But it doesn't accomplish His plan for the lost world in which we live. **Living FOR Christ** – "remaining" in Him – **is what makes all the difference.** As Believers, our commitment should begin at salvation and end when Jesus calls us home for our eternal reward. The words of Jesus reminded His Disciples that the game wasn't over when He went to the cross or even at the resurrection.

No matter your age or physical condition, if you "remain" in Christ, you can be fruitful. Why is that true? Because the promise in *John 15:5* is that IF we remain in Him and **He in us**, we will produce MUCH fruit. **There is no doubt about HIS part in the promise.** He continues to "remain", through the power of the Holy Spirit, in every Believer. The question that confronts each of us is, **"Are you committed to LIVE for Christ each and every day, no matter what you face?"**

Long-Term Effort

Is there any difference between commitment and effort? Consider the Christian couple who say they believe in marriage and are committed to their marriage. Yet they don't pray together or spend much free time together. They fail to deal with the small issues that crop up in marriage allowing those small things to grow into large problems. Now the marriage is in trouble. **Are they committed to marriage?** Perhaps yes, but are they expending the **effort** necessary to make the marriage fully fruitful? Seemingly, no.

See the difference between commitment and effort? BOTH are necessary for us as Followers of Christ to make a difference for the Kingdom. BOTH are vital to bearing fruit as we live for Christ.

> **Commitment is our mindset;
> Effort is our action.**

One drives the other. There would be **no effort** made to reach the world for Christ unless it is motivated by our **commitment** to sharing the Gospel of Christ with our lost friends and relatives.

> **Until we recognize the eternal value of what we share when we reach out with the Gospel, we will never make a serious effort to build our lives around that work.**

Once we commit ourselves to the task, why is it so important to maintain our effort long-term? Because it is that long-term labor that will yield "much fruit". I think the best way to illustrate the value of long-term effort for the Kingdom is to use a financial illustration:

Suppose you **deposit $10,000** in a bank account earning 4% compounding interest (don't you wish!) at age 20. **You leave the account untouched**, allowing the interest to accumulate. At age 30, you would have earned **$4,918** in interest, plus your original deposit. But what if you leave it for another

10 years? From age 30 to 40, you'd add another **$7,336** in interest. Another decade, from age 40 to 50 adds an additional **$10,945.** Wow! One more 10-year term, from age 50 to 60 increases your total by **$16,327**, meaning the value of your original $10,000 deposit is now worth $49,526.

What I hope you take away from the illustration is that the interest earned on the original investment **increases dramatically over time**. You would have earned **more than three times** the interest in the 4th decade than in the first. That's the power of compounding interest.

So, what if we apply the same principle to our lives as Followers of Jesus? Let's say you give your life to Christ at age 20 and commit to following Him. You serve faithfully, accomplishing what you can for a decade. Then another. And another. And finally, a fourth decade of service. While you may have been led to believe you become increasingly LESS valuable to the kingdom as you age, I'd like to submit that your knowledge of the Word and your walk with Christ is like compounding interest.

> **Every year you serve Christ has the potential to yield an ever-increasing benefit to the Kingdom!**

Because of your faithfulness, you become potentially **more** valuable every year for kingdom causes. Can I support that idea in Scripture? Let's look at this familiar passage and perhaps see it with **new eyes**:

> *He told many stories in the form of parables, such as this one: "Listen! A farmer went out to plant some seeds. As he scattered them across his field, some seeds fell on a footpath, and the birds came and ate them. Other seeds fell on shallow soil with underlying rock. The seeds sprouted quickly because the soil was shallow. But the plants soon wilted under the hot sun, and since they didn't have deep roots, they died. Other seeds fell among thorns that grew up and choked out the tender plants. Still other seeds fell on fertile soil, and* **they produced a crop that was thirty, sixty, and even a hundred times as much as had been planted!** *Anyone with ears to hear should listen and understand."   Matthew 13:3-9 NLT*

While this often-preached "Parable of the Sower" has many lessons for us, I want to focus on the fruit-bearing part of the story. We learn later in the chapter when Jesus openly explains the parable to His disciples that **the seed is the Word of God**, and we're reminded that not every seed will fall on fertile, prepared soil. But when the seed DOES bear fruit, there can be a significant difference in crop yield – some **30x**, some **60x**, and some even **100x**. Did you ever wonder what makes the difference? Have you ever been encouraged by your pastor to be a 100x believer and thought, "How do I do that?"

Remember the illustration about compounding interest? Recall that the longer the investment remains, the greater the return.

> **Isn't it possible that the key to understanding the different yields in the Parable is based on LONGEVITY?**

When we come to a saving knowledge of Christ's sacrifice for us and yield our lives to Him, we begin to earn "interest". The longer we serve our Savior, the greater the return on our account. So it benefits the Kingdom to have you **serve well, serve faithfully, and serve as long as you can**!

As a young Follower of Christ, I was completely "sold out". I worked hard and did what I could to share the truth of the Gospel with anyone who would listen. My life was fruitful. I served when and where I could and saw God bless my ministry efforts. Not every year has been as fruitful as it should have been, but that lack of productivity is my own failure and not that of the empowering Holy Spirit.

The Spirit of God continues to drive my commitment and, as I face my own 4th Quarter, I realize I must make sure my effort matches my commitment if I hope to fulfill my role in God's Kingdom plan. This book is a manifestation of that urgency I feel about serving God and finishing strong for Christ. I pray that YOUR passion for Christ results in your long-term commitment and effort for the Kingdom.

Long-Term Health

Commitment and effort can only be maximized when we are able to serve long enough to make a difference. Some Christians suffer from debilitating sickness or disease and may not be able to experience a full and fruitful life. None of us are completely able to escape the ravages of sin in our world. It is the presence of sin that causes sickness and disease. It is the presence of sin that shortens our effective ministry lives and prohibits us from achieving all we might otherwise accomplish.

> **While Jesus' death on the cross satisfied the penalty of sin in our lives, the presence of sin in our world still wreaks havoc on the redeemed as well as the lost.**

In spite of what some teach, death and disease are a result of sin, NOT a result of the failure of our faith. Scripture shows us that even in the age of the miracles found in the New Testament, not everyone was healed. The fall of man brought about the ravages of decay on all of creation:

> *Against its will, **all creation was subjected to God's curse**. But with eager hope, the creation looks forward to the day when it will join God's children in glorious freedom from death and decay. For we know that **all creation has been groaning** as in the pains of childbirth right up to the present time. And **we believers also groan**, even though we have the Holy Spirit within us as a foretaste of future glory, for **we long for our bodies to be released from sin and suffering**. We, too, wait with eager hope for the day when God will give us our full rights as his adopted children, including **the new bodies he has promised us**.*
> *Romans 8:20-23 NLT*

Sin yields its effects on us as we struggle with seemingly simple illnesses like colds and flu (either of which can still kill us) and more complex diseases like diabetes and cancer, and now even the ravages of a pandemic that has killed nearly 4 million people worldwide. Currently, more than **100 million Americans have diabetes or pre-diabetes!**[12] Globally, there are more than 18 million new cancer cases each year.[13] One hundred million Americans are considered **overweight or obese** and 10% of

---

[12] https://www.cdc.gov/media/releases/2017/p0718-diabetes-report.html

[13] https://www.who.int/cancer/PRGlobocanFinal.pdf

those are children over the age of six.[14] Have I made my point?

What does death and disease have to do with service to the Kingdom? If you get cancer and die, you're "out of the game". That's out of your control. But not all disease and sickness is out of our control.

> **We make choices that influence our availability to serve Christ.**

Sometimes, we make BAD choices that derail our opportunities to be of service to our Lord.

If you are too overweight or out of shape to serve as God intended, that's on you. If your body can't fight off disease because you've neglected yourself, that's at least partly your fault. If you can't control your body's cravings and you suffer physically for it, don't blame God. My goal in this section is NOT to beat up every Christian who has packed on a few pounds, or who doesn't take their medication like they should, or who doesn't eat right and get the rest required to function at peak mental and physical capacity. I have consistently been one of them, to my detriment.

---

[14] https://en.wikipedia.org/wiki/Obesity_in_the_United_States

> **But the game isn't over yet. It's just the 4th Quarter for me. I can still make a difference by recommitting myself to the principles of God.**

If I am to serve God to the fullest, I need to do better. I've already started my conditioning program. My first step was to change my mindset by focusing on eternal values. I need to see my body as the vehicle by which God will bring the Gospel to those who need to hear.

> *Don't you realize that **your body is the temple of the Holy Spirit**, who lives in you and was given to you by God? **You do not belong to yourself, for God bought you with a high price.** So you must **honor God with your body**. 1 Corinthians 6:19-20 NLT*

Read that again. You were purchased by the precious blood of Jesus lock, stock, and barrel. **You are not your own.** You aren't entitled to make your own choices about the health of your body any more than you are entitled to make your own choices about sin. God determines what is right and wrong. Don't blame your current condition on Him or "genetics". Perhaps you do have a predisposition to certain physical problems. Maybe you do have to work a lot harder than your friends to stay in shape. Do you require more sleep? Get it. Need to swear off sweets? Then do it. Wish you could stop smoking or vaping? Then don't just rely on your own willpower – that hasn't worked up to this point.

I won't drone on and on about what's wrong with you if you promise not to look at my picture on the back of the book and email me to tell me I'm overweight. We both know the score.

I WILL make some suggestions that I hope we can all live (longer) with to make us more available to the Savior who bought us. In no particular order:

- **Get enough sleep.** Not happening now? Maybe that's your reason for moodiness or fatigue or even depression. Did you know lack of sleep increases craving for carbohydrates? Make sure you don't have sleep apnea.

- **Take your medicine as directed.** Why would anyone go pay good money to a physician and then decide to self-diagnose? Do you really believe "Dr. Google" is smarter than your physician? If you do, then get a new doctor!

- **Eat right.** Sounds good until I decide to order a pizza and can't stop stuffing myself. Sugared soft drinks? Not a good idea. Lots of carbs? Not good either. Hate veggies? Too bad. Fiber gives you gas? At least I don't live with you!

- **Get enough exercise.** Now I'm just meddling, right? A recent Swedish study found that exercise is the number one contributor to longevity. That should be good enough to motivate you. But how much exercise is enough? Sources vary, but 2½ hours of moderate exercise, like brisk walking, each week is great. That averages out to 30 minutes x 5 days per week. Use the time to pray or dream or take along a partner and just chat.

- **Stay connected socially.** Join Facebook if you must, but connecting in person with living, breathing people is better. If you aren't already active in church, find one and get involved. If you belong, make sure you actively care about others so they will also care about you.

- **Focus on what gives your life meaning.** As a Christian, you shouldn't have a problem focusing on your role as a Believer. But other passions are important, too. Develop them. Always wanted to learn to paint? Then do it. Colonel Harlan Sanders of KFC fame got his first $99 Social Security check at age 65 and decided he needed to do something else to make some additional cash – and we got fried chicken! John Glenn went back into space at age 77. It's never too late to fulfill your life's dreams. **Just make sure you're also fulfilling God's plans.**

- **Plan for your future.** That might sound strange if you're reading this and you're 85 years old. But we all need to be looking forward, ready for whatever God places in front of us.

*I focus on this one thing: Forgetting the past and **looking forward to what lies ahead**, I press on to reach the end of the race and receive the heavenly prize for which God, through Christ Jesus, is calling us.*
Philippians 3:13-14 NLT

I once recommended to a patient that she undergo cataract surgery to improve her vision. I should mention that she was 104 years old. She responded, "But I'm too old." My response? "If God wants you to live to be 110, do you want to be able to see what's going on around you?" We must stay ready for what God has in store for us.

> **I fear that too often we give up on life before God is done using us.**

I posed this question in the introduction, so by now you might have forgotten it: **"What will be the last great work of your life before God calls you home?"** I challenge you to begin to dream about your answer. Maybe start praying about it on your 30-minute daily walks?

The apostle Paul understood the need to **"work as HARD as you can for as LONG as you can."** Just as he offered his life as an example for Timothy to follow, so we, too, can emulate his life of ministry. Paul had this to say the last time he saw the elders from the church at Ephesus:

> ***I have done the Lord's work humbly*** *and with many tears.* ***I have endured the trials*** *that came to me from the plots of the Jews.* ***I never shrank back from telling you what you needed to hear****, either publicly or in your homes. I have had one message for Jews and Greeks alike –* ***the necessity of repenting from sin and turning to God, and of having faith in our Lord Jesus.***
>
> *"And now I am bound by the Spirit to go to Jerusalem. I don't know what awaits me, except that the Holy Spirit tells me in city after city that* ***jail and suffering lie ahead****. But my life is worth nothing to me* ***unless I use it for finishing the work assigned me by the Lord Jesus*** *– the work of telling others the Good News about the wonderful grace of God. "And now I know that none of you to whom I have preached the Kingdom will ever see me again.* ***I declare today that I have been faithful.*** *Acts 20:19-26 NLT*

Paul worked hard; endured trials; didn't quit even when threatened by trials; and finished his ministry.

He was able to declare himself **faithful**. What will it take for you to be able to do the same?

> **What changes need to be made in your life so you can state like Paul, "I have been faithful."?**

No matter how long we get to serve our Lord, no matter what we face, if we have been faithful to our calling as Followers of Christ, we WILL hear,

> *"Well done, my good and faithful servant. You have been faithful...Let's celebrate together!"* Matthew 25:21 NLT

4th Quarter adults understand hard work and commitment. Our parents and grandparents "wrote the book on it" and passed down those values to us. We see in the pages of Scripture that the saints of old were completely committed to the plans and work of God for their whole lives. We are called to do the same. Don't stop dreaming and believing that God has more for you to do. Do your part. He's already done His.

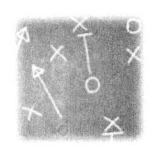

Final Thoughts

Coaching clichés are as much a part of the world of football as goalposts and helmets. You've likely heard most, if not all, of these:

> "You've got to give 110% on every play!"
>
> "Just leave it all on the field."
>
> "We need to take things one game at a time."
>
> "This game will be won or lost in the trenches."
>
> "Keep playing hard until the whistle blows."

I could spiritualize each of those clichés and I probably have somewhere in the pages of this book. There's good advice in each of them, but as Believers, the advice we really need to follow comes from the Holy Spirit, in this case through the words of Paul as he urged Timothy to live with meaning:

> **Pursue** *righteousness and a godly life, along with faith, love, perseverance, and gentleness.* **Fight** *the good fight for the true faith.* **Hold tightly** *to the eternal life to which God has called you,* **which you have declared so well before many witnesses**. *And I charge you before God...that you* **obey** *this command without wavering.* **Then no one can find fault**

with you from now until our Lord Jesus Christ comes again. *1 Timothy 6:11-14 NLT*

Whatever your age; no matter what you've done in the past for Christ, NOW is the BEST time to make the BIGGEST difference for the Kingdom of God. It's just the 4th Quarter. The game isn't over. "Keep playing hard until the whistle blows!"

The apostle Paul is such an amazing example of all the strategies in this book that I must close with his own 4th Quarter testimony:

> *Don't be afraid of suffering for the Lord.* **Work at telling others the Good News, and fully carry out the ministry God has given you.** *As for me, my life has already been poured out as an offering to God. The time of my death is near.* **I have fought the good fight, I have finished the race, and I have remained faithful. And now the prize awaits me** – *the crown of righteousness, which the Lord, the righteous Judge, will give me on the day of his return.* **And the prize is not just for me but for all who eagerly look forward to his appearing.** *2 Timothy 4:5-8 NLT*

Read that last sentence again, because the Holy Spirit doesn't want you to forget it. I pray you will **Finish Strong for Christ,** and may your legacy be even greater than your faith.

Questions to help you prepare for what God is going to do next in your life:

1. Are you confident you've passed from "death to life" through faith in Jesus Christ? If yes, then why?

2. If your faith is an **irrevocable gift** based on your hearing and believing the Gospel, how does that make you feel about your relationship with God?

3. How does it impact your life to know that you have **already** entered into an eternal existence through faith in Jesus – you already have eternal life?

4. When you look in the mirror, do you see an **Image-Bearer of the eternal God**? Why or why not?

5. If you could do **anything** for God in the next five years with **no fear** of failure or finances, what would it be?

6. Which do you value most, your time or your wealth and possessions?

   Now, which one do you think God wants you to yield to Him first?

7. How are you making sure your **Faith** will make a difference in others for the Kingdom **long after you're gone?**

8. Do you feel God's power and strength working through you as you serve Him? How?

9. Do you believe God has empowered you with a **speaking** or a **helping/serving gift**?

10. Of the seven gifts listed in Romans 12:6-8, which do you suspect is your **primary gift** and why?

11. How are you currently using your spiritual gift to benefit others and the Kingdom?

12. What is the difference between how the world views wealth and how the Bible views it?

13. Have you handled your finances up to this point in your life in a way that acknowledges your **stewardship** of what God has provided?

    If not, how do you intend to change?

14. Why do you think Jesus talked so much about money?

15. Do you have a **financial and giving plan** in place that will benefit others and the Kingdom after you're gone? If so, what?

16. What are some characteristics of the person(s) you'd like to find to **mentor**?

17. Paul understood that disciples need more than **knowledge about God**. What else do you believe your disciple should learn from **you**?

18. What kind of **spiritual legacy** do you hope to leave on those who are following you in life?

19. Can you imagine being able to impact eternity by leaving a **financial legacy** to further God's Kingdom plans? Why or why not?

20. **Why is longevity so important** for the lifetime impact on your fruitfulness for Christ?

21. Regarding your **long-term health**, what changes are you willing to make to be more useful and available for God's Kingdom plans?

22. Can you **list 3 things** that will be changing in your life as a result of recognizing your role **for** Christ and renewing your commitment **to finish strong** for Him?

Great Online Links for 4th Quarter Adults

Personal Faith:

https://www.amazon.com/James-Dickey/e/B07VXQWSGX - Author page for Dr. James Dickey

http://4thq.org/ - 4th Quarter Ministries

https://www.biblegateway.com/ - Bible Reading Program with various translations

https://thebibleproject.com/ - Bible Teaching and Instructional Videos

https://www.stchm.org/ - South Texas Children's Home and International Missions opportunities

https://www.crosswalk.com/ - Christian Devotionals and other Christian Living Information

https://www.imb.org/trips/ - International Mission Board – Southern Baptist Convention opportunities

https://jacobswalk.blogspot.com/ - Faith-based Teaching Blog

Travel (Not an endorsement of any company):

Holland America Cruise Line: https://www.hollandamerica.com/en_US.html

Southwest Airlines: https://www.southwest.com/

Allegiant Airlines: https://www.allegiantair.com/

National Park Service: https://www.nps.gov/planyourvisit/passes.htm

Mapquest Travel Information: https://www.mapquest.com/

Google Translate to translate foreign words and phrases: https://translate.google.com/

Financial (Not an endorsement of any company):

Smart Asset Retirement Guide Calculators: https://smartasset.com/retirement/

Donor Advised Fund Information: http://programforgiving.org/charitable/pages/home.jsp

Legal Zoom Estate Planning Information https://www.legalzoom.com/personal/estate-planning/estate-planning-bundle.html

Lifestyle:

Comparison Tool to evaluate communities: https://www.bestplaces.net/compare-cities/

National Weather Service: https://www.weather.gov/

Senior Living Information: https://www.seniorliving.org/leisure/top-senior-websites/

Made in the USA
Middletown, DE
10 June 2021